THE I ♥ WHOLE FOODS MARKET® COOKBOOK

101 Natural and Organic Meals That Won't Break the Bank

★ Andrea Lynn

Ulysses Press

Thanks to my many friends and family, who, along with giving me words of encouragement, lent their bellies for taste-testing needs.

Published by
Ulysses Press
P.O. Box 3440
Berkeley, CA 94703
www.ulyssespress.com

ISBN: 978-1-56975-983-7
Library of Congress Catalog Number 2011926027

Printed in the United States by Bang Printing

10 9 8 7 6 5 4 3 2 1

Acquisitions Editor: Keith Riegert
Project Manager: Kelly Reed
Managing Editor: Claire Chun
Editors: Lauren Harrison, Leslie Evans
Design and layout: what!design @ whatweb.com
Front cover photos: background © tomograf/istockphoto.com; grunge elements © edge69/istockphoto.com; olive and pomegranate © Nagendra Bhagwat/istockphoto.com
Recipes pictured on pages 9, 14, 19, 27, 32, 41, 47, 52, 57, 62, 69, 73, 79, 85, 89, 94, 101, 107, 113, 116, 120, 127, 131, 136 © Judi Swinks Photography
Food stylist for pictured recipes: Anna Hartman-Kenzler
Other interior photos: see page 141

Distributed by Publishers Group West

TABLE OF CONTENTS

Introduction 5

APPETIZERS & SNACKS 7

SALADS & SOUPS 22

SIDES 36

PASTA 55

POULTRY 70

MEAT 83

FISH & SHELLFISH 98

VEGETARIAN 110

DESSERTS 125

Recipe Index 142

About the Author 144

INTRODUCTION

Just walking into any Whole Foods Market makes me giddy with happiness. I love the freshness and variety of the produce, much of which is locally sourced and in season. The fish case displays a rainbow of seafood, and the bountiful meat counter contains cut after cut of glorious meat. The bakery has freshly baked mini brioche and French bread, the salad bar is stocked with goodies, and the prepared food aisle offers drool-worthy choices, like marinated goat cheese.

Shopping at Whole Foods makes me feel excited about the meals I'm planning and informed about the food I choose to put into my body. However, one thing I don't love is the dollar sign that comes at the register. There's a price to pay for quality, and Whole Foods can do some damage to your wallet.

However, there are ways to lessen the load of a hefty grocery bill. The I Love Whole Foods Market Cookbook aims to keep the advantages of shopping at Whole Foods while adding some cost-cutting techniques to the mix. One guiding principle is to balance out meat and fish dishes with plenty of less-expensive grains and vegetables. This reduces the grocery bill and results in a better-balanced diet. You can also check Whole Foods's weekly circular online before you make your shopping list. If possible, stock up on nonperishables like canned items and bulk dry goods during a sale and then use them at a later date. For specialty items that you only need a little of, the salad bar is a great place to find inexpensive small quantities of a variety of ingredients. All the recipes in this book can be made with items from Whole Foods, and while every ingredient may not be available under the Whole Foods or 365 Everyday Value brands, the store's high-quality standards make it easy to know you're getting the best of the best.

You'll find simple ideas like this throughout these chapters to get you through any occasion—delectable appetizers to excite your guests, vegetable-centered meals for the health-conscious, and meat and seafood dishes that are great any night of the week. The 101 recipes that follow are inspired by cuisines from around the world and will help you take advantage of all that Whole Foods has to offer while keeping your food budget under control.

RECIPE ICONS

For easy identification, the recipes in this book are labeled with handy icons to meet your needs. Need dinner on the table fast? Look for Quick & Easy dishes. Budget Friendly icons will be especially easy on the wallet, and Vegetarian and Vegan icons will help you find meatless meals in a snap.

Vegetarian

Vegan

Quick & Easy

Budget Friendly

APPETIZERS & SNACKS

Think you need to make appetizers or snacks just for special occasions? Think again. They are a fun and flavorful way not only to start a meal but also to make great snacks throughout the day or for a light lunch. For example, cherry tomatoes dipped in hummus is a common afternoon snack at my home, and spring rolls are often a lunch indulgence.

And then, of course, it's great to have a few appetizer recipes in your repertoire to serve when company comes. A flavorful appetizer doesn't have to be complicated. Often, a good recipe merely combines a few complementary ingredients, transforming them into magic. The good selection of fresh quality produce at Whole Foods makes it a great starting point for simple yet flavorful appetizers. Also, while most of the recipes in this chapter require minimal prep work, they have plenty of spark to wake up your taste buds.

SPRING ROLLS

With scallions, basil, and hoisin, you can pack a lot of flavor into a small spring roll wrapper. The soft, creamy avocado provides a great contrast to the crunch of the carrots and radishes. Hard-to-find Asian products like hoisin sauce and spring roll wrappers are easy to find at Whole Foods. Spread a little of the sauce in each roll or serve it on the side for dipping—or do both!

½ English cucumber, peeled
1 medium carrot
6 radishes
2 scallions
1 (10.5-ounce) package spring roll wrappers
2 tablespoons hoisin sauce, plus more to serve
12 basil leaves
1 avocado, sliced (see sidebar)

Position a box grater in a medium bowl. Grate the cucumber, carrot, and radishes into the bowl. Chop the scallions and add to the bowl. Stir together. Blot the vegetables with paper towels to absorb excess moisture. Fill another medium bowl with cold water. Individually soak each spring roll wrapper in cold water for 15 to 30 seconds until pliable. Place the wrapper on a work surface. Spread ½ teaspoon hoisin sauce in a line down the center of the wrapper. Fill with 1 basil leaf, 1 slice of avocado, and 1½ tablespoons filling. Roll the wrapper over the mixture once, then fold in the sides. Continue tightly rolling the spring roll, just like you would a burrito. Repeat for the remaining wrappers. Serve with additional hoisin sauce.

TO PEEL AN AVOCADO:

Halve the avocado. Sink a sharp knife into the seed and pull it out. Holding one half of the avocado in the palm of your hand, insert a large spoon under the avocado flesh, next to the peel, and run it all around the avocado until you can lift the whole avocado half out of the peel.

Yield: 10 to 12 spring rolls *Prep Time:* 15 minutes

ARUGULA AND SALAMI–STUFFED PEPPADEW PEPPERS

Peppadew peppers are a sweet pepper soaked in a pickling brine, giving them a sweet-and-sour appeal. You can get them from the Whole Foods olive bar.

10 Peppadew peppers from the Whole Foods olive bar, drained

3 to 4 tablespoons ⅓ less fat cream cheese (neuchâtel)

1 teaspoon canola oil

3 tablespoons chopped salami

1 (5-ounce) package arugula

Arrange the peppers on a plate. Fill each pepper with about 1 teaspoon cream cheese. Heat the canola oil in a medium nonstick sauté pan or skillet over medium-high heat. Add the salami and cook, stirring constantly, 1 to 2 minutes. Add the arugula and cook, stirring constantly, until wilted, 2 to 4 minutes. Remove from the heat. Fill each pepper with an equal portion of the salami arugula mixture. Serve.

Yield: 10 peppers | *Prep Time:* 5 minutes | *Cooking Time:* 5 minutes

CURED SALMON WITH HORSERADISH CREAM AND CRACKERS

Smoked salmon (called lox) is one of my favorite indulgences, but there's no arguing that it's expensive! It's much cheaper to prepare cured salmon, called gravlax, which isn't nearly as difficult as it sounds. The salmon just sits in a mixture of salt, sugar, and pepper for two days, and voilà! Serve with horseradish cream and crackers for a delightful appetizer.

1½ cups kosher salt

1 cup sugar

2 tablespoons black peppercorns

1 pound Whole Foods organic salmon fillet

1 cup 365 Everyday Value Organic Low Fat Sour Cream

1 tablespoon prepared horseradish

crackers, as needed

2 tablespoons chopped chives (optional)

Combine the salt, sugar, and peppercorns in a small bowl. Place the salmon in a glass dish and pat the salt mixture into all exposed sides of the salmon. Cover with foil and place cans on top to weigh it down. Refrigerate for 48 hours.

Remove the salmon from the salt mixture, and rinse away any salt that clings to the fish. Cut the salmon into thin slices. Mix the sour cream and horseradish in a small bowl. To serve, spread crackers with the sour cream mixture, top with slices of the cured salmon, and sprinkle with chives.

Yield: 1 pound *Prep Time:* 15 minutes, plus 2 days in fridge

ROASTED TOMATO BRUSCHETTA

For the most part, it's considerably cheaper to do your own slicing and chopping than to buy anything prepared from Whole Foods. Except for the crostini. It's just a few cents more than a loaf of French bread and a load easier when making something like bruschetta. But if you're inclined to make your own crostini, just thinly slice a loaf of French bread and toast for 10 minutes in a 375°F oven until slightly crisped.

- 2 pints grape tomatoes
- 4 cloves garlic, peeled
- 1 tablespoon extra-virgin olive oil
- ½ teaspoon kosher salt
- ¼ teaspoon freshly ground black pepper
- 1 container Whole Foods Crostini
- 2 tablespoons chopped basil

Preheat the oven to 425°F. Line a rimmed baking sheet with foil. Spread the tomatoes and the garlic on the prepared baking sheet. Drizzle with the olive oil and sprinkle with the salt and pepper. Toss to coat with the olive oil and seasonings. Roast until the tomatoes are crinkly and collapsed, 25 to 30 minutes, turning the baking sheet once halfway through cooking. Set aside to cool. Use your hands to combine the tomatoes and the garlic. Taste the spread and adjust the seasoning, if needed. To serve, spread the tomato mixture onto each crostini and garnish with the basil.

Yield: About 20 *Prep Time:* 5 minutes *Cooking Time:* 25 to 30 minutes

SHRIMP WITH SPICY COCKTAIL SAUCE

Cocktail sauce is a snap to make and gives a wallop of taste that's not apparent with the jarred variety.

1 cup 365 Everyday Value Organic Tomato Ketchup

1½ tablespoons prepared horseradish

1 teaspoon grated lemon zest

1 tablespoon freshly squeezed lemon juice

2 teaspoons hot sauce, like Sriracha

1 pound Whole Foods peeled cooked shrimp

Combine the ketchup, horseradish, lemon zest, lemon juice, and hot sauce in a medium bowl. Taste the sauce and adjust the ingredients, as needed. Serve with the cold cooked shrimp.

Yield: 4 servings *Prep Time:* 5 minutes

HUMMUS WITH CUCUMBER SLICES AND CHERRY TOMATOES

In this hummus recipe, the traditional component tahini is left out. It's not a mistake—tahini (sesame paste) is a little expensive, and when I buy it, it usually lingers in the fridge because not many other recipes call for tahini. That's why it was deliberately omitted from this recipe, and the (slightly nontraditional) hummus shines without it. Serve with pita wedges and/or vegetable slices.

2 cloves garlic, coarsely chopped

1 (15-ounce) can 365 Everyday Value Organic Garbanzo Beans, rinsed and drained, plus 1 tablespoon liquid reserved

grated zest and juice of 1 lemon

1 teaspoon sweet paprika

kosher salt and freshly ground black pepper

¼ cup extra-virgin olive oil, more or less

2 cucumbers, sliced

1 pint cherry tomatoes

pita bread, quartered, to serve (optional)

fresh parsley, for garnish (optional)

In a food processor, puree the garlic, chickpeas, reserved chickpea liquid, lemon zest, lemon juice, paprika, ½ teaspoon salt, and ¼ teaspoon pepper. With the food processor running, pour in the olive oil through the feed tube, and process until emulsified. Taste the hummus, and adjust the salt and lemon juice, if needed. Top with an extra drizzle of olive oil, a sprinkle of paprika, and parsley, if using. Serve with cucumber slices, tomatoes, and pita, if using.

Yield: 4 servings *Prep Time:* 5 minutes

BACON-WRAPPED BANANAS

Pretty much anything is better when it's wrapped in bacon. The sweetness of the cooked bananas makes them a particularly good candidate for a bacon wrap.

$

3 medium firm bananas

1 tablespoon brown sugar

1 teaspoon cayenne pepper

1 teaspoon kosher salt

6 to 8 slices 365 Everyday Value Uncured Center Cut Smokehouse Bacon, Reduced Sodium

Preheat the oven to 400°F. Place one rack 3 inches from the broiler and another in the middle. Line a rimmed baking sheet with foil. Peel each banana and cut diagonally into 4 or 5 pieces about 2 inches long. Combine the brown sugar, cayenne, and salt in a small bowl, and sprinkle the mixture onto the banana pieces. Cut the bacon strips into thirds or long enough to wrap around a banana piece. Wrap each banana piece, secure with a toothpick, and place on the prepared baking sheet. Cook in the middle of the oven until the bacon is beginning to caramelize, 15 to 20 minutes. Remove from the oven, and preheat the broiler. Broil the bananas until the bacon is fully caramelized, just 2 to 3 minutes, checking carefully to make sure it doesn't burn. Serve.

Yield: 16 to 20 pieces *Prep Time:* 10 minutes *Cooking Time:* 20 to 25 minutes

BLACK-EYED PEA DIP

Black-eyed peas bring good luck on New Year's, but this dip can be enjoyed any time of year. The roasted tomatoes add a lot of depth.

1 pint grape tomatoes, halved

½ small red onion, coarsely chopped

1 tablespoon extra-virgin olive oil

1 jalapeño chile, seeded and chopped

1 roasted red bell pepper, chopped

1 (15-ounce) can 365 Everyday Value Black-Eyed Peas, rinsed and drained

1 tablespoon freshly squeezed lemon juice

1 tablespoon chopped cilantro

kosher salt and freshly ground black pepper

365 Everyday Value Lightly Salted Tortilla Chips with Sunflower and Flax Seeds Multigrain, as needed

Preheat the broiler. Line a rimmed baking sheet with foil, and add the tomatoes and onion. Drizzle the olive oil over, tossing to coat. Broil until semicharred, 4 to 5 minutes, watching closely to prevent burning. Meanwhile, combine the jalapeño, bell pepper, black-eyed peas, lemon juice, and cilantro in a medium bowl. Add the tomatoes and onions to the bowl. Stir to combine and season to taste. Serve with chips.

Yield: 4 servings *Prep Time:* 10 minutes *Cooking Time:* 5 minutes

CHEESE LOG WITH APPLE SLICES

Cheddar cheese and apple is a classic pairing. Spreading this cheese log onto apple slices is a nice way to contrast the creaminess of the softened cheese with the crisp bite of apple.

¼ pound sharp cheddar cheese, coarsely chopped

1½ ounces ⅓ less fat cream cheese (neuchâtel)

1 scallion, coarsely chopped

2 teaspoons Worcestershire sauce

½ cup walnuts, chopped, divided

apples, such as Granny Smith, Gala, or Red Delicious, as needed

Add the cheddar cheese, cream cheese, scallion, Worcestershire sauce, and ¼ cup walnuts to a food processor. Pulse until smooth, about 1 to 2 minutes, stopping once to scrape down the mixture. Transfer the cheese mixture to waxed paper, and mold into a log shape. Sprinkle on the remaining ¼ cup walnuts. Wrap the entire log in waxed paper, and refrigerate for a few hours. Serve with apple slices.

Yield: 4 servings *Prep Time:* 15 minutes, plus time to refrigerate

GUACAMOLE WITH POMEGRANATE SEEDS

Homemade guacamole is so easy to make and much tastier than the store-bought kind. You can find pomegranate seeds in the produce section; they add a healthy crunch to this guac.

- 2 ripe avocados, diced (see page 8)
- 2 tablespoons chopped cilantro
- 1 scallion, finely chopped
- juice of ½ lime
- ½ teaspoon kosher salt
- ¼ cup pomegranate seeds
- 365 Everyday Value Lightly Salted Tortilla Chips with Sunflower and Flax Seeds Multigrain, as needed

In a small bowl, mash the avocado using a fork. Add the cilantro, scallion, lime juice, salt, and half the pomegranate seeds and mix. Garnish with the remaining pomegranate seeds, and serve with tortilla chips.

Yield: 4 servings *Prep Time:* 5 minutes

CARAMELIZED ONION DIP

I love caramelized onions. The caramelization process brings out their natural sweetness. Be patient—don't brown the onions too quickly— and you'll be justly rewarded.

1½ tablespoons canola oil
4 cups chopped yellow onions (1½ pounds)
½ teaspoon kosher salt
2½ tablespoons low-fat mayonnaise
3 tablespoons crème fraîche
2 teaspoons freshly squeezed lemon juice
chips or crackers, to serve

Heat the canola oil in a large sauté pan or skillet over medium-high heat. Add the onions and salt, coating in the oil. Decrease the heat to medium-low, and cook the onions, stirring every couple of minutes. Monitor the onions to ensure they caramelize but do not burn. If the onions are cooking too quickly, decrease the heat. Let the onions cook about 25 minutes. Off-heat, add the mayo, crème fraîche, and lemon juice, stirring to combine. Taste the dip and adjust the ingredients as needed. Transfer to a bowl, cover, and refrigerate for several hours. Serve with chips or crackers.

Yield: 4 servings *Prep Time:* 5 minutes, plus time to refrigerate *Cooking Time:* 30 minutes

SALADS & SOUPS

Canned soups are so convenient that some cooks have forgotten how delicious a bowl of homemade soup can be. Simmering a pot of soup on the stove allows all the fresh flavors to meld in a way that can't come from a can. Soup brings back comforting memories of childhood and can be an easy way to comfortably explore new cuisines. Another reason soup is a pleasure to make is the ease of cooking it—you don't have to worry much about overcooking or undercooking.

Salads are another menu item that it's easy to get lazy about. Sure, you can fill your vegetable quota by grabbing a bag of premixed salad greens and dumping bottled dressing on top. If you spend a little extra time mixing fresh ingredients, you will be rewarded with some really delicious results. It's easy to fall into a salad rut, so the recipes in this chapter add a little variety that will banish the humdrum.

PANZANELLA SALAD

One of my favorite salads, panzanella is a salad from Italy centered on tomatoes, olives, and bread cubes soaked in salad dressing. If you're not the kind of person who likes to sop up leftover sauce with bread, this might not be your salad. Instead, substitute mini mozzarella balls (ciliegine) for the bread cubes.

1 teaspoon 365 Everyday Value Organic Dijon Mustard

kosher salt

1 tablespoon red wine vinegar, plus more as needed

2½ tablespoons extra-virgin olive oil, plus more as needed

2 cucumbers, peeled and cut into bite-size pieces

5 Roma tomatoes, cut into bite-size pieces

¼ cup pitted kalamata olives, or any olive of your choice from the Whole Foods olive bar, coarsely chopped

1 large handful basil leaves (about 25 to 30 leaves)

2 cups bite-size cubes day-old firm bread, like French or Italian bread from a Whole Foods bakery

Make the salad dressing: Add the mustard, ½ teaspoon salt, and vinegar to a small bowl. Whisk until combined, then drizzle in the olive oil, whisking to emulsify. Taste and adjust the salt, vinegar, and olive oil, as needed.

In a large bowl, add the cucumbers, tomatoes, olives, and basil. Pour half the salad dressing into the bowl, and toss with the salad mixture. Top the salad with the bread cubes and pour the remaining salad dressing over the bread. Let the salad sit for 15 to 20 minutes before serving, so the bread cubes have time to absorb the dressing. Toss the salad to distribute the bread cubes, and serve.

Yield: 4 servings *Prep Time:* 20 minutes, plus 20 minutes to sit

CORN SALAD

Fresh corn is a thing of beauty, but getting those kernels off the cob isn't. One of my favorite tools in the summer is OXO's Corn Stripper, and I swear they don't pay me to endorse it. What normally takes me 15 minutes to accomplish is done in just a few seconds with the Corn Stripper. Roasted red bell peppers can be found either in a Whole Foods olive bar or in the prepared foods aisle.

6 ears corn, shucked
kosher salt and freshly ground black pepper
¼ cup coarsely chopped cilantro
¼ cup finely chopped red onion
1 pint grape tomatoes, cut in half
2 Whole Foods roasted red bell peppers, diced
juice of 1 lime
1½ tablespoons extra-virgin olive oil

In a large pot of salted boiling water, cook the ears of corn until the kernels have turned bright yellow, about 3 to 4 minutes. Drain and let cool. When cool enough to handle, remove the corn kernels from the cob using a knife. Put the corn in a large bowl, and add the cilantro, red onion, tomatoes, bell peppers, ½ teaspoon salt, ¼ teaspoon pepper, lime juice, and olive oil. Toss the salad, taste, and adjust the seasonings as needed. Serve.

Yield: 4 servings *Prep Time:* 15 minutes *Cooking Time:* 5 minutes

SPRING GREENS SALAD

This is a nice basic salad with a simple homemade dressing and a sprinkle of sunflower seed kernels. Salad dressing is so easy to make there's no reason to settle for store-bought. For an ingredient you don't use often, like sunflower seed kernels, it's cheaper and easier to nab just the amount you need from the Whole Foods salad bar than to buy a large bag.

1 teaspoon 365 Everyday Value Organic Dijon Mustard

2 teaspoons honey

kosher salt

1½ tablespoons 365 Everyday Value Organic Apple Cider Vinegar, plus more as needed

4 tablespoons extra-virgin olive oil, plus more as needed

1 (9-ounce) bag spring greens

4 Roma tomatoes, chopped

2 carrots, grated

2 medium fennel bulbs, trimmed of feathery stalks and thinly sliced

1 cucumber, peeled and chopped

1 ripe avocado, chopped (see page 8)

2 tablespoons sunflower seed kernels

Make the salad dressing: In a small bowl, add the mustard, honey, salt, and vinegar. Whisk until combined, then drizzle in the olive oil, whisking to emulsify. Taste and adjust the salt, vinegar, and olive oil, as needed.

In a large bowl, add the greens, tomatoes, carrots, fennel, cucumber, and avocado. Lightly toss to combine. Drizzle with some of the dressing, toss, and taste, repeating until the ingredients are just coated. Sprinkle with the sunflower seed kernels and serve.

Yield: 4 servings *Prep Time:* 15 minutes

LENTIL SALAD WITH MANGO

Because of their small size, fiber-rich lentils are great at absorbing other flavors. The bright flavors of mango, onion, and cilantro combine in this invigorating salad.

1 (17.63-ounce) package Melissa's Steamed Ready-to-Eat Lentils (available in refrigerated part of produce section)

1 cup diced mango (about 1 large mango; see sidebar)

1½ tablespoons chopped red onion

¼ cup chopped cilantro

½ teaspoon kosher salt

¼ teaspoon freshly ground black pepper

½ tablespoon freshly squeezed lemon juice

1 tablespoon extra-virgin olive oil

In a medium bowl, add the lentils, mango, onion, cilantro, salt, and pepper. Toss to combine. Drizzle with the lemon juice and the olive oil and toss again. Serve.

TO PEEL A MANGO:

Slice through the mango lengthwise, next to one side of the flat pit, and detach; repeat for the other side. Spoon out the flesh and chop or slice as needed.

Yield: 4 servings *Prep Time:* 10 minutes

CHINESE CHICKEN SALAD

With its large helping of chicken, this salad can serve as a healthy main course. The presence of orange in both the dressing and the salad nicely brings the whole dish together, which is also bolstered by the crunch of water chestnuts.

juice of 2 oranges

2 tablespoons soy sauce

2 teaspoons poppy seeds

1 tablespoon honey

2 tablespoons extra-virgin olive oil

½ medium head red cabbage, thinly sliced

1 head romaine lettuce, chopped

2 scallions, chopped

1 cucumber, peeled and chopped

1 avocado, diced (see page 8)

1 (8-ounce) can sliced water chestnuts, rinsed and drained

1 (11-ounce) can mandarin oranges, drained

3 cups shredded cooked chicken (from a Whole Foods rotisserie chicken)

Make the dressing: In a small bowl, whisk the orange juice, soy sauce, poppy seeds, and honey until combined. Continue whisking, slowly adding the olive oil, until emulsified. Reserve until needed.

Combine the cabbage and lettuce in a large bowl. Add the scallions, cucumber, avocado, water chestnuts, mandarin oranges, and chicken. Toss to combine. When ready to serve, toss with the dressing.

Yield: 4 servings *Prep Time:* 15 minutes

SOUP WITH GREENS

Just a little bacon is all that's needed to add oomph to this soup chockfull of healthy leafy green vegetables. To get a nice flavor, make sure to choose a variety of greens.

$

2 slices bacon, diced

1 medium onion, diced

2 cloves garlic, minced

3 cups chopped combined greens (spinach, collards, turnip greens, Swiss chard, or others)

8 cups 365 Everyday Value Organic Chicken Broth

kosher salt and freshly ground black pepper

In a large pot over medium-high heat, add the bacon, and stir until cooked but not crisp, 4 to 6 minutes. Add the onion and cook, stirring, until translucent, 2 to 3 minutes. Add the garlic and the greens, and cook briefly until the garlic is golden and the greens are wilted, 1 to 2 minutes. Add the chicken broth, and season to taste with salt and pepper. Increase the heat to high, and bring the soup to a boil. Reduce the heat, and simmer until the flavors have melded, about 15 to 20 minutes.

Carefully transfer half of the soup to a food processor. Puree until smooth, about 1 minute. Return the pureed soup to the pot. Season to taste, and reheat the soup, if necessary. Serve.

Yield: 4 servings | *Prep Time:* 10 minutes | *Cooking Time:* 30 minutes

CHICKEN SOUP WITH CRISPY RICE

When I was a child, my mom went to a cooking class and learned how to make chicken soup with crispy fried rice. It was such a mess frying the rice in a vat of hot oil—splatter everywhere. We made it only once, but the sultry chicken broth with crispy rice grains haunted me for years. Then I found Whole Foods frozen rice. The individual grains are frozen in a way that a quick stint in a sauté pan gives the same results I remember from childhood.

$

6 cups 365 Everyday Value Organic Chicken Broth

kosher salt and freshly ground black pepper

4 Whole Foods organic, free-range boneless, skinless chicken thighs

1 (20-ounce) bag frozen 365 Everyday Value Organic Whole Grain Brown Rice

2 tablespoons canola oil

⅓ cup chopped scallions

In a medium pot over high heat, add the chicken broth, ½ teaspoon salt, and ¼ teaspoon pepper and bring to a boil. Season the chicken thighs and add to the boiling broth. Cover and reduce the heat to low. Simmer until the chicken is cooked through, 25 to 30 minutes. Cut into the thickest chicken piece to check that it's no longer pink. Take the pot off the heat, and transfer the chicken thighs to a plate to cool. Shred the chicken with a fork, or cut into pieces. Return to the soup.

When ready to serve, heat the soup. Heat the canola oil in a large nonstick skillet over high heat. Add one-half of the rice in one layer in the pan. Cook, undisturbed, until the rice is golden and crispy, 4 to 5 minutes. Transfer the rice to a plate. Add the remaining rice to the pan, and cook undisturbed for 3 to 4 minutes (the second batch will cook faster). To serve, ladle the chicken soup into bowls. Garnish with the crispy rice and the scallions.

Yield: 4 servings *Prep Time:* 15 minutes *Cooking time:* 45 minutes

POTATO LEEK SOUP

Creamy potato soup is always a treat, and benefits here from the addition of leeks. Vegetarian Better Than Bouillon No Chicken Base (available in an 8-ounce container) is a good, cheap substitute for the vegetable broth used in this recipe.

1 tablespoon unsalted butter

3 medium leeks, sliced ¼ to ½ inch thick (see sidebar)

3 cups 365 Everyday Value Organic Vegetable Broth

1 pound red potatoes, diced

kosher salt and freshly ground black pepper

2 tablespoons crème fraîche

1 teaspoon dried dill, for garnish (optional)

Melt the butter in a medium pot over medium-high heat. Add the leeks and cook, stirring occasionally, until soft, about 10 minutes. Add the vegetable broth, potatoes, ½ teaspoon salt, and ½ teaspoon pepper, and bring to a boil. Lower the heat to medium-low and cook until the potatoes are tender and the soup is thickened, 25 to 30 minutes. Remove from the heat and, if you would like, use an immersion blender to puree the soup. Season to taste, and stir in the crème fraîche. Ladle the soup into bowls and garnish with dill, if using.

TO CLEAN LEEKS:

Cut off the tough green leaves and the tip of the root end. Transfer to a bowl of cold water and swish the leeks vigorously to loosen the layers and remove any dirt. Leaf through the layers to see whether any soil remains. If needed, drain and repeat.

Yield: 4 servings *Prep Time:* 15 minutes *Cooking time:* 45 minutes

GARAM MASALA TOMATO SOUP WITH CHEESY FLATBREAD

The addition of garam masala—which is a combo of spices like cumin, coriander, cardamom, and cloves—gives this tomato soup a unique twist. Why do I call for whole tomatoes in this recipe and then make you puree them, rather than starting out with a puree? Well, cans of whole tomatoes contain the best ratio of tomato to tomato juice, which will result in a better soup. Note: Baking soda is added to the soup to reduce the acidity of the tomatoes. Don't be concerned if it causes a brief bubbling.

- 2 teaspoons extra-virgin olive oil
- 2 cloves garlic, minced
- ¼ teaspoon cayenne pepper
- 1 tablespoon garam masala, plus more as needed
- 2 (28-ounce) cans peeled whole plum tomatoes, including juice
- ¾ teaspoon kosher salt
- 1 tablespoon unsalted butter
- ¼ cup heavy cream
- ½ teaspoon baking soda
- 2 to 3 flatbreads or pita breads, halved
- ¼ cup Whole Foods Grated Parmigiano-Reggiano cheese

Heat the olive oil in a Dutch oven or a large pot over medium-high heat. Add the garlic, cayenne pepper, garam masala, and salt, stirring constantly, until the seasonings are fragrant, about 30 seconds. Add the tomatoes and ½ teaspoon salt. Bring to a boil, cover, reduce the heat, and cook at a constant simmer until the flavors have melded, about 20 minutes. Add the butter and the cream, and stir to combine. Remove from the heat and let cool. Use an immersion blender or a food processor to puree the soup. Taste the soup and adjust the seasonings, if necessary. Sprinkle the baking soda over the soup, and stir to combine.

Preheat the broiler. Line a rimmed baking sheet with foil, and add the flatbread halves. Sprinkle with a good amount of cheese. Broil until the edges of the flatbreads are golden, 2 to 3 minutes, watching closely so the bread doesn't burn. Serve with the hot soup.

Yield: 4 servings | *Prep Time:* 5 minutes | *Cooking Time:* 25 minutes

TURKEY CHILI WITH BEANS

Chili always makes for a hearty, satisfying meal. When it's made with ground turkey and beans, it's a healthy, complete meal in one pot. Serve the chili with your favorite garnishes, such as sour cream, shredded cheese, olives, diced avocado, or thinly sliced scallions.

$

2 teaspoons canola oil

1 pound ground dark meat turkey

2 yellow onions, finely chopped

2 red bell peppers, finely chopped

1 (28-ounce) can chopped tomatoes, including juice

1 (15½-ounce) can 365 Everyday Value Organic Pinto Beans, not drained

1 (15½-ounce) can 365 Everyday Value Organic Black Beans, not drained

¾ cup strongly brewed coffee

1 tablespoon chili powder, plus more as needed

3 cloves garlic, chopped

kosher salt and freshly ground black pepper

In a Dutch oven over medium-high heat, heat the canola oil, add the turkey and cook, stirring constantly to break up the meat into small pieces, until cooked, 6 to 8 minutes. Add the onion and the bell pepper, sautéing until soft, 5 to 7 minutes. Add the tomatoes, beans, and coffee, stirring to combine. Bring the mixture to a simmer, and add the chili powder, garlic, ¾ teaspoon salt, and ½ teaspoon pepper. Lower the heat to medium-low, cover, and cook at a constant simmer, until the flavors have melded, 30 to 45 minutes. Taste and adjust the seasonings. Ladle the chili into bowls and serve with garnishes.

Yield: 4 servings | *Prep Time:* 10 minutes | *Cooking Time:* 1 hour

KIMCHI SOUP WITH CELLOPHANE NOODLES

This soup is perfect for the days of winter when you're all sniffly. The comfort of soup combined with the spiciness of the kimchi to clean your sinuses will put you on the path to recovery. Add the noodles to individual bowls of soup; adding them to the entire pot will allow them to soak up too much broth.

6 cups 365 Everyday Value Organic Vegetable Broth

1½ to 2 cups kimchi, such as Not My Mother-in-Law's Kimchi, cut into bite-size pieces

1 (8-ounce) can sliced water chestnuts, rinsed and drained

1 (15-ounce) can baby corn, rinsed and drained

½ (14-ounce) package 365 Everyday Value Organic Firm Tofu, cut into 1-inch pieces

1 (3¾-ounce) package cellophane noodles, soaked in hot water for 10 minutes

2 scallions, chopped

Heat the broth in a medium pot over medium-high heat. Add the kimchi to the broth, using more or less, as you prefer. Add the water chestnuts, corn, and tofu. Let the soup cook until the flavors have melded, about 5 minutes. To serve, ladle the soup into bowls and garnish with the cellophane noodles and the scallions.

Yield: 4 servings *Prep Time:* 10 minutes *Cooking Time:* 10 minutes

SIDES

Sometimes, a great side dish makes the meal. Turkey is all right, but Thanksgiving is really all about the array of delicious sides like stuffing and sweet potatoes. Not every night can be as special as Thanksgiving, but serving a thoughtful, delicious side can make any meal more memorable.

This chapter features new, healthier spins on comforting favorites, like mashed potatoes with the tang of buttermilk and creamed spinach with just a spoonful of crème fraîche to give a hint of creaminess. With these, there are also some dishes that might be less familiar, like cucumber briefly sautéed with pepper flakes and celery root plus apple made into a puree. And why reserve side dishes for second glory? Combine a few and feast on them to make a meal.

PESTO-STUFFED TOMATOES

As far as I'm concerned, you can never go wrong with pesto, Parmesan, or panko. I use all three together for these simple and sultry stuffed tomatoes.

2 tablespoons Whole Foods Grated Parmigiano-Reggiano cheese

⅓ cup panko bread crumbs

1 tablespoon fresh Whole Foods Pesto

4 small to medium tomatoes, hulled (see sidebar)

Preheat the oven to 400°F. Combine the cheese and the bread crumbs in a small bowl. Add the pesto, and stir to combine with the dry ingredients. Fill each tomato's cavity with the bread crumb mixture. Place the tomatoes in an ovenproof dish and bake until the tomatoes and the filling are hot and the top is browned, about 15 minutes.

TO HULL A TOMATO:

Using a small paring knife, core the tomatoes, leaving a round opening. With a spoon or a melon baller, scoop out the insides, including the seeds. Don't scoop too close to the bottom or the tomatoes won't stay sturdy. Rinse the tomatoes with water and place them upside down to drain on a paper towel.

Yield: 4 servings | *Prep Time:* 5 minutes | *Cooking Time:* 15 minutes

POLENTA WITH DRIED MUSHROOMS

While I chose the black trumpet mushrooms for this recipe, Whole Foods has a substantial selection of dried mushrooms. Choose your favorite. Because the dark mushroom stock is used to heighten the earthy flavor of the polenta, the shade is a bit murky—great to eat but not photo-worthy.

½ ounce dried black trumpet mushrooms
1½ cups hot water
2 cups milk
½ teaspoon dried thyme
½ teaspoon kosher salt
½ cup coarse cornmeal
1½ tablespoons unsalted butter

Soak the dried mushrooms in the water for 15 minutes. Drain the mushrooms through a fine-mesh strainer set over a 2-cup measure, and reserve the soaking liquid. Rinse the mushrooms, chop them, and reserve. Pour 1 cup of the soaking liquid into a medium pot, through the strainer again to make sure there's no dirt left. Add the milk, thyme, and salt, and bring to a boil over high heat. Add the cornmeal, whisking constantly. Turn down the heat, and let simmer until the polenta is as thick as you want it, 5 to 10 minutes. Stir in the reserved mushrooms and the butter. Taste and adjust the seasonings if necessary. Serve.

Yield: 4 servings *Prep Time:* 15 minutes *Cooking Time:* 20 minutes

LOW-FAT CREAMED SPINACH

Using reduced-fat versions of both cream cheese and Greek yogurt greatly reduces the fat in this recipe. The result isn't as creamy as a full-fat creamed spinach, but it still tastes very rich and the yogurt gives it a pleasing tang.

2 (16-ounce) bags frozen 365 Everyday Value Chopped Spinach, thawed

½ cup water

4 cloves garlic, minced

4 ounces ⅓ less fat cream cheese (neuchâtel)

½ cup milk

½ cup 2% Fage Greek yogurt

kosher salt and freshly ground black pepper

In a large pot over medium-high heat, cook the spinach in the water, stirring occasionally, until all the water evaporates, about 5 minutes. Stir in the garlic and cook 1 minute. Reduce the heat to low, and add the cream cheese and the milk, stirring and cooking, until the cream cheese is melted, 5 to 7 minutes. Remove from the heat and stir in the yogurt. Season with salt and pepper, and serve.

Yield: 6 servings *Prep Time:* 5 minutes *Cooking Time:* 10 minutes

MARINATED EGGPLANT WITH OLIVES

This simple marinated eggplant recipe makes a nice Mediterranean-influenced warm-weather side. It's cheaper to buy the olives from Whole Foods olive bar, so you can purchase just the amount you need, and not a whole jar which might languish in the fridge. The quality and variety are better, too.

3 medium Italian eggplants, sliced crosswise ½-inch thick

extra-virgin olive oil, as needed

kosher salt and freshly ground black pepper

¼ cup chopped mint

⅓ cup Whole Foods oil-cured black olives, pitted and coarsely chopped

Preheat the broiler. Line one or two rimmed baking sheets with foil, and add the eggplant. Drizzle with olive oil and season with salt and pepper. Broil the eggplant until slightly charred but still chewy, 3 to 4 minutes; turn the eggplant over and broil again 3 to 4 minutes. Remove from the broiler, and let cool. Repeat until all the eggplant has been broiled. When the eggplant has cooled, cut into bite-size pieces. Transfer to a bowl, and combine with the mint and the olives. Season with salt and pepper, and drizzle with olive oil. Serve the marinated eggplant cold or at room temperature.

Yield: 4 servings *Prep Time:* 20 minutes, plus at least 1 hour to marinate *Cooking Time:* 20 minutes

CELERY ROOT AND APPLE PUREE

Never made celery root before? Trust me, you're missing out. Celery root has a flavor that resembles celery and parsley and a texture that's similar to a potato or a parsnip. This dish is like mashed potatoes for those who think potatoes are a little bland.

2 pounds celery root, peeled and cut into 1-inch pieces

kosher salt

2 red apples, peeled and sliced

2 tablespoons unsalted butter

½ cup half-and-half

Add the celery root to a pot of salted water, and set over high heat. When the water reaches a boil, add the apples and cook until the celery root is easily pierced with a knife, about 12 minutes. Reserving 1 cup of the cooking water, drain the celery root and apples and place in a food processor. Add the butter, half-and-half, and ½ teaspoon salt. Puree until smooth, scraping down the sides if necessary. If you want a smoother consistency, add the reserved cooking water as needed. Serve at once.

Yield: 4 servings *Prep Time:* 10 minutes *Cooking Time:* 25 minutes

ROASTED BRUSSELS SPROUTS WITH MUSTARD SEEDS

Brussels sprouts sometimes get a bad rap, but they're one of my favorite vegetables. My favorite way to prepare Brussels sprouts is to roast them because the process brings their natural sweetness to the surface.

- 1¼ pounds Brussels sprouts, ends trimmed and halved lengthwise
- 2½ tablespoons extra-virgin olive oil, divided
- 1 tablespoon freshly squeezed lemon juice
- kosher salt and freshly ground black pepper
- 1½ teaspoons mustard seeds

Preheat the oven to 400°F. Line a rimmed baking sheet with foil. Add the Brussels sprouts, and cover with 1½ tablespoons olive oil, lemon juice, ½ teaspoon salt, and ¼ teaspoon pepper. Toss to combine. Roast the sprouts until the outer leaves are crisped, about 45 minutes, rotating the baking sheet once midway through. Remove from the oven, and add the remaining 1 tablespoon olive oil and the mustard seeds. Toss to combine with the sprouts. Taste and adjust the seasonings as needed. Serve.

Yield: 4 servings *Prep Time:* 5 minutes *Cooking Time:* 45 minutes

QUICK-SAUTÉED CUCUMBERS WITH RED PEPPER FLAKES

I bet you never thought of cooking cucumbers, right? Neither did I, but one of my favorite Szechuan restaurants briefly sautés cucumbers to better infuse them with red pepper flakes. Just try it, and you'll be adding cooked cucumbers to your repertoire, too. The key to this recipe is to just briefly cook the cucumbers over high heat.

2 tablespoons extra-virgin olive oil

2 teaspoons red pepper flakes

2 cloves garlic, minced

1-inch piece fresh ginger, grated

3 English cucumbers, peeled, cut in half lengthwise, and cut into 1-inch pieces

1 tablespoon soy sauce

Heat the olive oil in a large sauté pan or skillet over high heat. Add the pepper flakes, garlic, and ginger, and sauté, stirring constantly, until fragrant, 15 to 30 seconds. Add the cucumber, stirring constantly to combine with the remaining ingredients, about 1 minute. Add the soy sauce, and continue stirring for 1 more minute, scraping up any bits of goodness that have stuck to the bottom. Serve.

Yield: 4 servings *Prep Time:* 10 minutes *Cooking Time:* 5 minutes

BUTTERMILK MASHED POTATOES

Substituting low-fat buttermilk for milk and cream cuts down on calories while adding a lovely tang. Peel the potatoes if you wish, but you'll also be peeling away a lot of their nutritional value.

2 pounds russet potatoes (about 4 large potatoes)

kosher salt

2 tablespoons unsalted butter

¾ to 1 cup low-fat buttermilk

2 tablespoons chopped chives (optional)

Fill a large pot halfway with water. Chop the potatoes into medium pieces, as equal in size as possible. Add 1 teaspoon salt, and more water if necessary to cover the potatoes. Bring to a boil over high heat. Cook until the potatoes are tender (stick a knife into a potato to check), 12 to 15 minutes. Drain the potatoes, and return to the pot. Add ¾ teaspoon salt, butter, and ¾ cup buttermilk. Use a potato masher to mash the potatoes until smooth, adding more buttermilk, if needed, for desired consistency. Taste and season with more salt, if needed, and garnish with chives, if using. Serve.

Yield: 4 servings *Prep Time:* 15 minutes *Cooking Time:* 15 minutes

COUSCOUS WITH DRIED CRANBERRIES AND PINE NUTS

Couscous is a cinch to make but can be a little boring if you cook it in water. Using vegetable stock, or some other kind of broth, gives it a much richer flavor. The addition of pine nuts and cranberries makes this a well-rounded side that you'll be happy to eat on a regular basis.

2 teaspoons canola oil

¼ cup pine nuts

2 cups 365 Everyday Value Organic Vegetable Broth

kosher salt and freshly ground black pepper

1 cup couscous

⅓ cup dried cranberries

2 scallions, coarsely chopped

Heat the canola oil in a medium pot over medium-high heat. Add the pine nuts. Stirring constantly, toast the pine nuts, cooking until lightly browned, 2 to 3 minutes. Add the vegetable stock, ½ teaspoon salt, and ¼ teaspoon pepper. Bring to a boil, and add the couscous and the cranberries. Remove from the heat and cover with a lid. Let sit for 10 minutes. Fluff the couscous, and stir in the scallions. Taste and adjust the seasoning as needed. Serve.

Yield: 4 servings *Prep Time:* 5 minutes *Cooking Time:* 15 minutes

SMASHED "FRIED" POTATOES

"Fried" is a misnomer here because the crispiness of the smashed potatoes comes from a stint in the oven, so this recipe is both easier to make and healthier to consume than one involving frying. Win, win.

8 medium red potatoes (about 1½ pounds)
kosher salt and freshly ground black pepper
extra-virgin olive oil

Add the potatoes and 1 teaspoon salt to a large pot, and fill ¾ full of water, making sure to cover the potatoes. Bring to a boil over high heat, and cook the potatoes until almost tender, about 30 minutes. Drain and let cool.

Preheat the oven to 450°F. Line a rimmed baking sheet with foil. When the potatoes are cool enough to handle, halve lengthwise. Place the potato halves cut-side up on the prepared baking sheet. Using a potato masher, gently press down on the potatoes to flatten. (You don't want to press so hard that the potatoes break into a million pieces. Just press gently to flatten them.) Generously dress with olive oil, salt, and pepper. Roast the potatoes until slightly browned and crispy on top, about 30 minutes. Serve.

Yield: 4 servings *Prep Time:* 5 minutes *Cooking Time:* 1 hour

KASHA WITH SPRING VEGETABLES

Whole Foods is a mecca of seasonal, hard-to-find produce. For example, in late spring, you'll find fiddleheads (the furled fronds of a young fern). It's always fun to incorporate new delights into your dinner. Some of these treasures can get expensive, so it's best to buy just a small amount of them to incorporate into a larger dish with a grain like kasha. Kasha is whole-grain buckwheat, popular in Eastern Europe. It's a source of fiber, protein, magnesium, and manganese.

$

2 teaspoons extra-virgin olive oil

1 (10-ounce) bag fresh spinach

1 zucchini, grated on a box grater

½ cup fiddleheads, or other seasonal vegetable

2 cups 365 Everyday Value Organic Chicken Broth or Vegetable Broth

1 cup Wolff's Kasha

kosher salt and freshly ground black pepper

Heat the olive oil in a medium pot over medium-high heat. Add the spinach, in batches if necessary, and stir until wilted. Add the zucchini and the fiddleheads, sautéing until softened and combined with the spinach, 2 to 3 minutes. Add the broth, kasha, ½ teaspoon salt, and ¼ teaspoon pepper. Bring to a boil, cover, and reduce the heat to low. Simmer until the kasha is tender, about 15 minutes. Remove from the heat, and fluff the kasha with a fork. Taste and adjust the seasoning as needed, and serve.

Yield: 4 servings | *Prep Time:* 5 minutes | *Cooking Time:* 30 minutes

CURRIED CAULIFLOWER WITH DRIED CHERRIES

Cauliflower is an underrated vegetable. It has a subtle taste that allows it to pick up surrounding flavors and is the perfect choice for this pairing with curry powder and dried cherries.

1 tablespoon unsalted butter

2 teaspoons curry powder

kosher salt and freshly ground black pepper

1 large head cauliflower, cut into bite-size pieces

⅓ cup water

¼ cup dried cherries

Melt the butter in a large sauté pan or skillet over medium-high heat. Add the curry powder, ½ teaspoon salt, and ¼ teaspoon pepper, and cook, stirring, until fragrant, 30 seconds. Add the cauliflower, and stir to combine with the butter and spices. Cook until slightly golden, 2 to 3 minutes. Add the water and dried cherries, and cover with a lid. Cook until the cauliflower is tender and the water has evaporated, 3 to 4 minutes longer. Taste and adjust the seasonings as needed. Serve.

Yield: 4 servings *Prep Time:* 5 minutes *Cooking Time:* 10 minutes

BRAISED FENNEL WITH ORANGES AND OLIVES

The licorice-like flavor of fennel makes for an intriguing combination with briny olives and sweet oranges. The cheapest option for buying the olives is to purchase just the amount you need from the Whole Foods olive bar.

$

1 tablespoon extra-virgin olive oil

3 fennel bulbs, trimmed of feathery stalks and quartered

1¼ cups 365 Everyday Value Organic Chicken Broth or Vegetable Broth

juice of 1 orange

¼ cup Whole Foods oil-cured black olives, pitted

½ teaspoon kosher salt

¼ teaspoon freshly ground black pepper

1 tablespoon unsalted butter

Heat the olive oil in a large sauté pan or skillet over high heat. Add the fennel, cut-sides down. Cook, undisturbed, until the fennel browns, 2 to 3 minutes. Add the broth, orange juice, olives, salt, and pepper. Cover with a lid, and reduce the heat to medium-low so the liquid is still heartily simmering. Cook until the fennel is tender, 20 to 25 minutes. Transfer the fennel to a plate, then increase the heat to high. Let the liquid boil until it reduces significantly, about 2 minutes. Remove from the heat, add the butter, stir to melt, and pour over the fennel. Serve.

Yield: 4 servings *Prep Time:* 5 minutes *Cooking Time:* 30 minutes

ROASTED ASPARAGUS WITH ORANGE ZEST

I always look forward to asparagus season in the spring. Asparagus is often at its best when it's simply prepared, but I think it benefits from the addition of a little orange flavor.

2 bunches asparagus, trimmed (see sidebar)
1½ tablespoons extra-virgin olive oil
grated zest and juice of 1 orange
kosher salt and freshly ground black pepper

Preheat the oven to 400°F. Line a rimmed baking sheet with foil, and add the asparagus in rows. Drizzle with the olive oil and the orange juice. Sprinkle with salt and pepper. Roast until the asparagus is tender, about 20 minutes. Garnish with the orange zest, and serve.

TO TRIM ASPARAGUS:

The tough end of the asparagus needs to be removed before you eat it, but don't worry—Mother Nature makes it easy for you. Just bend the bottom part of the asparagus, about 1 to 2 inches from the bottom, and the stalk will snap at the point where tender meets tough. Go through a handful of asparagus at a time for ease.

Yield: 4 servings *Prep Time:* 5 minutes *Cooking Time:* 20 minutes

CILANTRO BROWN RICE

Brown rice is very healthy but often makes for a pretty boring side dish. Here, it's given a huge boost of flavor from cilantro, scallions, lime, and avocado. Even better, enhancing the flavor is hardly any work at all.

1 cup brown rice
1 bunch cilantro leaves
1 avocado, chopped (see page 8)
2 scallions, coarsely chopped
juice of 1 lime
1 clove garlic, crushed
kosher salt
1 tablespoon extra-virgin olive oil

In a medium pot, cook the brown rice according to the package instructions. Meanwhile, puree the cilantro, avocado, scallions, lime juice, garlic, and ½ teaspoon salt in a food processor. Pour the olive oil through the feed tube and puree until smooth, about 1 to 2 minutes. When the rice is tender, drain, and return to the pot. Add the cilantro seasoning to the rice, and stir to combine. Taste and adjust the salt as needed. Serve.

Yield: 4 servings *Prep Time:* 15 minutes *Cooking Time:* 30 to 45 minutes

PASTA

Who doesn't like to sit down to a plateful of pasta? It's versatile and affordable, and feels like a complete meal in one dish. Pick a pasta shape, a protein, and a vegetable and meld the components into a meal. Pasta has become a global food, so you can pull flavors from any continent into a pasta dish. Tomatoes combine with chickpeas and spices for an Indian flair; soy sauce, snow peas, and sesame oil mix together in an Asian homage to pasta salad. And whether you make a baked pasta dish that slowly brings the components together or a quickly cooked one that picks up the bright notes around it, pasta is all about tying together an array of flavors. Whole Foods is a good source for fresh ingredients, like the eggplants and ramps that you'll find in this chapter, and also sells a very decent jarred marinara sauce under its 365 Everyday Value brand. While I think the pasta selected in each recipe works well with the sauce and other ingredients, if you hate capellini and love fettuccine, follow your heart—because that's what cooking is about.

ASIAN-STYLE FUSILLI SALAD

This pasta salad is a big hit every time I make it. It's great as an appetizer or as lunch but can also be a light warm-weather entrée.

1 pound 365 Everyday Value Fusilli
4 tablespoons toasted sesame oil
3 tablespoons honey
3 tablespoons soy sauce
2 tablespoons balsamic vinegar
½ cup low-fat mayonnaise
kosher salt and freshly ground black pepper
1 teaspoon canola oil
2 red bell peppers, chopped
1½ cup broccoli florets
2 cups snow peas
3 scallions, thinly sliced
sesame seeds, as needed

Cook the pasta in large pot of boiling salted water until tender but still firm to the bite, stirring occasionally. Drain very well. Transfer to a large bowl. In a small bowl, whisk the sesame oil, honey, soy sauce, vinegar, and mayonnaise until blended. Season to taste with salt and pepper. Mix half of the dressing into the pasta. Heat the canola oil in a large heavy sauté pan or skillet over medium-high heat. Add the bell peppers and broccoli, cooking until just tender, about 5 minutes. Add the snow peas and toss with the vegetables. Sauté until the snow peas are tender, just 1 minute. Add to the pasta. Season to taste with salt, and add the remaining dressing, stirring all to combine. Garnish with the scallions and sesame seeds, and serve at room temperature.

Yield: 4 servings *Prep Time:* 10 minutes *Cooking Time:* 12 minutes

FETTUCCINE WITH LEMON SHRIMP

Shrimp doesn't need a lot of assistance. This simple dish of pasta, shrimp, lemon, and cheese has a somewhat indulgent simplicity.

1 pound Whole Foods Market Organic Fettuccine

3½ tablespoons extra-virgin olive oil, divided, plus more as needed

grated zest and juice of 2 lemons

½ cup Whole Foods Grated Parmigiano-Reggiano cheese

1 (16-ounce) bag frozen Whole Foods Farm-Raised Uncooked Shrimp, thawed

kosher salt and freshly ground black pepper

2 cloves garlic, minced

Cook the pasta in large pot of boiling salted water until tender but still firm to the bite, stirring occasionally. Meanwhile, make the lemon sauce: In a medium bowl, combine 3 tablespoons olive oil, lemon zest, lemon juice, and cheese. Set aside. Drain the pasta in a colander, reserving ¼ cup pasta water. Return the pasta to the pot, toss with a drizzle of olive oil, and keep hot.

Season the shrimp with salt and pepper. Heat ½ tablespoon olive oil in a large sauté pan or skillet over medium-high heat. Add the shrimp and garlic and sauté until the shrimp is pink, 2 to 3 minutes. Remove from the heat. Add the reserved pasta and pasta water to the pan with the shrimp along with the lemon sauce, stirring to mix. Taste and adjust the seasonings as needed. Serve.

Yield: 4 servings | *Prep Time:* 5 minutes | *Cooking Time:* 20 minutes

SPAGHETTI AND MEATBALLS

In today's health-conscious world, ground turkey is often preferred to beef, but it doesn't really deliver the same heartiness. Here, turkey and beef are combined in a compromise that delivers a less fatty meatball that's still full of rich meaty flavor.

$

1 pound 365 Everyday Value Spaghetti

½ pound Whole Foods organic dark meat ground turkey

½ pound Whole Foods organic ground beef, 90 percent lean

1 teaspoon kosher salt

¼ teaspoon freshly ground black pepper

2 teaspoons Worcestershire sauce

1 large egg

¼ cup panko bread crumbs

1 tablespoon dried parsley flakes

1 (25-ounce) jar 365 Everyday Value Classic Marinara Pasta Sauce

1 tablespoon unsalted butter

Whole Foods Grated Parmigiano-Reggiano cheese, as needed

Cook the pasta in large pot of boiling salted water until tender but still firm to the bite, stirring occasionally. Drain in a colander, reserving ¼ cup pasta water, toss with a drizzle of olive oil, and reserve.

Make the meatballs: Preheat the oven to 425°F. Line a rimmed baking sheet with foil, and spray the foil with cooking spray. In a large bowl, combine the turkey, beef, salt, pepper, Worcestershire sauce, egg, bread crumbs, and parsley. Using a spoon or your hands, mix until combined. Form each meatball by rolling about 1 tablespoon of the mixture into a ball and placing on the prepared baking sheet. You should have about 30 meatballs. Bake until cooked through, about 15 minutes.

Meanwhile, heat the marinara sauce and butter in a large pot over medium-high heat. Let simmer so the flavors mingle, about 10 minutes. When the meatballs are ready, add to the sauce, and let cook 5 minutes longer. Add the reserved pasta to the meatballs and sauce. Thin the sauce with the pasta water if needed. Simmer until the pasta is hot, and serve garnished with Parmesan.

Yield: 4 servings | *Prep Time:* 15 minutes | *Cooking Time:* 30 minutes

ZUCCHINI PESTO PASTA

Pesto doesn't need to be made with basil—zucchini does double-duty in this recipe: Grated, sautéed zucchini is featured, and raw zucchini is used for the pesto. Light and fresh, this pasta feels like summer any time of year.

1 pound Whole Foods Market Organic Capellini

extra-virgin olive oil, as needed

4 medium to large zucchini, divided

2 medium cloves garlic, smashed

½ cup walnuts

½ cup Whole Foods Grated Parmigiano-Reggiano cheese

kosher salt and freshly ground black pepper

Cook the pasta in a large pot of boiling salted water until tender but still firm to the bite, stirring occasionally. Drain in a colander, reserving ¼ cup pasta water, toss with a little olive oil, and reserve.

Meanwhile, make the pesto: Coarsely chop 1½ zucchini and put in a food processor. Add the garlic, walnuts, cheese, ¼ teaspoon salt, and ¼ teaspoon pepper and puree. Pour ¼ to ½ cup olive oil through the feed tube, and puree until the mixture is emulsified. Taste and adjust the seasonings as needed.

Position a box grater in a large bowl, and grate the remaining 2½ zucchini. Heat 1½ tablespoons olive oil in a large sauté pan or skillet over medium-high heat. Add the grated zucchini and season with salt and pepper. Sauté the zucchini until tender, 3 to 5 minutes. Reduce the heat to low, and add the reserved pasta, pasta water, and pesto, stirring to combine. Simmer until the pasta is hot. Taste, adjust the seasonings as needed, and serve.

Yield: 4 servings | *Prep Time:* 5 minutes | *Cooking Time:* 25 minutes

SPINACH-STUFFED SHELLS

Tofu is oh-so-subtly added to these shells to give your diet an added protein boost without all the fat of excess cheese.

¾ (12-ounce) box jumbo pasta shells

2 teaspoons extra-virgin olive oil

14 ounces 365 Everyday Value Organic Soft Tofu, chopped

1 egg

12 ounces Whole Foods fresh mozzarella, shredded, divided

¾ teaspoon kosher salt

½ teaspoon freshly ground black pepper

1 teaspoon garlic powder

1 tablespoon dried parsley flakes

1 (25-ounce) jar 365 Everyday Value Organic Marinara Sauce, divided

½ (16-ounce) bag frozen 365 Everyday Value Chopped Spinach, thawed

Cook the pasta in a large pot of boiling salted water until tender but still firm to the bite, stirring occasionally. Drain in a colander, drizzle with the olive oil, and reserve. Make the spinach stuffing: In a large bowl, add the tofu, egg, half of the mozzarella, salt, pepper, garlic powder, parsley flakes, and ¾ cup marinara sauce. Squeeze the excess liquid from the spinach, add to the bowl, and mix.

Preheat the oven to 350°F. Place the reserved pasta shells in a 9 x 13-inch baking dish. Using a spoon, fill each shell with spinach stuffing. When finished, sprinkle the remaining cheese on the shells, then pour the remaining marinara sauce over the shells. Bake until warmed through, about 30 minutes. Serve.

Yield: 4 servings *Prep Time:* 15 minutes *Cooking Time:* 30 minutes

TURKEY LASAGNE

Garfield isn't the only one who loves lasagne. This turkey-based version of the popular Italian staple is great for a big crowd or to give yourself a couple days of leftovers.

$

2 teaspoons canola oil

1 pound Whole Foods organic dark meat ground turkey

½ kosher salt and ¼ teaspoon freshly ground black pepper

1 (25-ounce) jar 365 Everyday Value Roasted Garlic Pasta Sauce

1 (15-ounce) container 365 Everyday Value Part-Skim Ricotta Cheese

1 egg

½ cup grated zucchini

½ cup grated carrot

1 (16-ounce) box 365 Everyday Value No Boil Lasagne Noodles (12 noodles will be needed)

1 (12-ounce) package 365 Everyday Value Low-Moisture Part-Skim Shredded Mozzarella Cheese

Preheat the oven to 375°F. Heat the canola oil in a medium saucepan over medium-high heat. Add the ground turkey, salt, and pepper and sauté, stirring occasionally, until the turkey is fully cooked, about 8 minutes. Remove from the heat and stir in three-fourths of the pasta sauce. In a medium bowl, combine the ricotta, egg, grated zucchini, grated carrot, and remaining pasta sauce.

Add 1 to 2 tablespoons ricotta sauce to a 9 x 13-inch glass baking dish. Top with 4 noodles and all but 1 cup of the turkey sauce. Sprinkle 1 cup mozzarella cheese on top of the sauce. Layer with 4 more noodles. Add all but 1 cup of the ricotta sauce and top with 4 noodles. Combine the remaining ricotta sauce and turkey sauce and spread over the noodles. Sprinkle the remaining mozzarella on top. Cover the dish with foil, and bake until the noodles are easily pierced with a knife, about 45 minutes. Remove the foil and cook for 15 minutes longer, until the cheese is golden. Cut the lasagne into serving pieces and serve.

Yield: 6 servings *Prep Time:* 20 minutes *Cooking Time:* 1 hour

LINGUINE WITH TOMATOES AND EGGPLANT

You want to use a nonstick pan for this recipe. Eggplants are like sponges, they'll just keep soaking up all the olive oil that you use, so it's healthier and easier to use a nonstick pan.

1½ teaspoons olive oil

2 medium eggplants, peeled and chopped into small pieces

1 (25-ounce) jar 365 Everyday Value Organic Marinara Sauce with Eggplant

kosher salt and freshly ground black pepper

1 pound 365 Everyday Value Organic Whole Wheat Linguine

Whole Foods Grated Parmigiano-Reggiano cheese (optional)

Make the sauce: Heat the olive oil in a large nonstick sauté pan or skillet over medium-high heat. Add the eggplant, and cook, stirring occasionally, until slightly soft, 10 to 12 minutes. Add the marinara sauce, and stir to combine with the eggplant. Reduce the heat to low, cover the pan, and let simmer until the eggplant pieces are soft, 30 to 35 minutes. Season to taste with salt and pepper.

Meanwhile, cook the pasta in a large pot of boiling salted water until tender but still firm to the bite, stirring occasionally. Drain in a colander. Add the pasta to the sauce, and warm until the pasta is hot. Top with cheese, if using, or pass at the table.

Yield: 4 servings | *Prep Time:* 10 minutes | *Cooking Time:* 50 minutes

MEYER LEMON CARBONARA

With bacon, eggs, and cheese, this might not be the healthiest recipe in the book, but sometimes you need a classic Italian comfort dish. The Meyer lemons add a bit of a sweet and tart flavor.

$

2 tablespoons extra-virgin olive oil

¼ pound bacon, chopped

1 pound 365 Everyday Value Spaghetti

2 large eggs

⅔ cup Whole Foods Grated Parmigiano-Reggiano cheese

zest of 3 Meyer lemons and juice of 2 Meyer lemons

½ teaspoon kosher salt

¼ teaspoon freshly ground black pepper

2 cloves garlic, chopped

2 tablespoons chopped parsley

Heat the olive oil in a large sauté pan or skillet over medium heat. Add the bacon and cook until slightly crisp, 8 to 10 minutes. Remove and drain on paper towels. Leave the olive oil and bacon fat in the pan and keep hot over very low heat. Cook the pasta in a large pot of boiling salted water until tender but still firm to the bite, stirring occasionally.

When the pasta is almost ready, whisk together the eggs, cheese, lemon zest, lemon juice, salt, and pepper in a bowl. Drain the pasta and reserve ½ cup of the pasta water. Cook the garlic in the bacon fat for 1 minute, then add the pasta to the pan. Stir the pasta to heat and to coat. Remove the pan from the heat. Pour the egg mixture into the pasta and toss rapidly with tongs or a large fork so that the eggs thicken but don't scramble. Once the eggs have thickened, you can add some of the pasta water until the sauce reaches the desired consistency. Garnish with parsley, and serve.

Yield: 4 servings | *Prep Time:* 10 minutes | *Cooking Time:* 20 minutes

SPAGHETTI WITH EGGS AND RAMPS

Ramps are an early spring vegetable, beloved along the East Coast. This dish highlights their exciting flavor, but if you're really in the mood and it's not ramp season, scallions are a good substitute.

1 pound 365 Everyday Value Spaghetti
extra-virgin olive oil, as needed
25 to 30 ramps, greens and whites separated
4 eggs
Whole Foods Grated Parmigiano-Reggiano cheese

Cook the pasta in a large pot of boiling salted water until tender but still firm to the bite, stirring occasionally. Drain in a colander, reserving ½ cup pasta water, toss with a little olive oil, and reserve.

In a large nonstick sauté pan or skillet, heat 2½ tablespoons olive oil. Add the ramp whites. Cook, stirring occasionally, until fragrant, 1 to 2 minutes. Add the eggs and fry until the whites are set (without flipping). Remove from the heat. Add ramp greens, reserved pasta water, and pasta. Stir until the pasta is hot and well-coated with egg yolk. Garnish with cheese, and serve.

Yield: 4 servings *Prep Time:* 5 minutes *Cooking Time:* 25 minutes

CHEESE RAVIOLI WITH BACON AND PEAS

The peas add a bright vegetable flavor that cuts through the fattiness of the bacon and cheese.

$

1 (22-ounce) package frozen 365 Everyday Value Organic Cheese Ravioli

4 slices 365 Everyday Value Uncured Center Cut Smokehouse Bacon, Reduced Sodium, diced

½ (16-ounce) package frozen 365 Everyday Value Organic Green Peas

½ cup 365 Everyday Value Organic Chicken Broth or Vegetable Broth

kosher salt and freshly ground black pepper

Cook the pasta in a large pot of boiling salted water until tender but still firm to the bite, stirring occasionally. Drain and reserve.

Meanwhile, sauté the bacon in a large sauté pan or skillet over medium-high heat, stirring occasionally, until crisp, about 7 minutes. Transfer the bacon to a paper towel–lined plate. Discard all but 2 teaspoons of the bacon fat in the pan, and heat the remainder over high heat. Add the peas and the broth, cooking the peas until bright green and slightly softened, 2 to 3 minutes. Add the ravioli and the bacon back into the pan, and combine with the peas. Season to taste with salt and pepper, and serve.

Yield: 4 servings *Prep Time:* 5 minutes *Cooking Time:* 25 minutes

ANGEL HAIR WITH TOMATOES AND CHICKPEAS

With cumin, coriander, and cardamom, this pasta dish delivers an Indian spin on an Italian tomato sauce. If you want to rely entirely on pantry staples, you can substitute 1 tablespoon of dried basil for the fresh variety and make this dish without another trip to the store.

2 tablespoons extra-virgin olive oil

2 cloves garlic, minced

1 tablespoon ground cumin

1 tablespoon ground coriander

½ teaspoon ground cardamom

¼ teaspoon red pepper flakes

2 (15-ounce) cans 365 Everyday Value Organic Garbanzo Beans, rinsed and drained

1 (28-ounce) can peeled whole plum tomatoes, including juice

½ cup chopped fresh basil

kosher salt and freshly ground black pepper

1 pound Whole Foods Market Organic Capellini

Make the sauce: Heat the olive oil in a large sauté pan or skillet over medium heat. Add the garlic, cumin, coriander, cardamom, and pepper flakes, and stir constantly, until the oil is fragrant and somewhat darker, 1 to 2 minutes. Stir in the chickpeas. Add the tomatoes, breaking up with a spoon. Simmer, stirring occasionally, until slightly thickened, about 20 minutes. Stir in the basil and season to taste with salt and pepper.

Meanwhile, cook the pasta in a large pot of boiling salted water until tender but still firm to the bite, stirring occasionally. Drain the pasta and serve with the sauce ladled over the top.

Yield: 4 servings *Prep Time:* 10 minutes *Cooking Time:* 20 minutes

POULTRY

Poultry is a staple of the typical health-conscious carnivore's diet. A good source of protein and lower in fat than beef and pork, poultry is an easy choice. Sticking with organic, vegetarian-fed, antibiotic-free chickens like the ones at Whole Foods means you can have your poultry and feel extragood about it. Of course, organic chicken costs a bit more, but there are still ways to save money. First, buy dark meat instead of white, and enjoy the added benefit of extra flavor and moistness. Instead of purchasing pieces of chicken already butchered and trimmed of fat, buy a whole one, and ask the Whole Foods butcher to cut it into pieces for no extra cost. Also, look at Whole Foods circulars and their website for sales, as they often have bargains on chicken. Buy more than you need, and store it in the freezer. Add the warmth of cinnamon and comfort of apples to the traditional roasted chicken, utilize the cheapness of turkey drumsticks for an homage-to-Thanksgiving meal, and let fruit salsa adorn and pep up the usual sautéed chicken breast.

CINNAMON-SCENTED ROASTED CHICKEN WITH APPLES

Cinnamon is known as a dessert ingredient but can also be a great addition to savory dishes. It adds warmth to this braised dish. And here's a tip: Removing the backbone from the chicken shortens the cooking time.

$

3 Red Delicious apples, sliced

2 tablespoons unsalted butter, at room temperature

2 teaspoons grated orange zest (about 1 orange)

1 teaspoon ground cinnamon

½ teaspoon kosher salt

¼ teaspoon freshly ground black pepper

1 (3¼ to 3½-pound) Whole Foods organic, free-range chicken

Preheat the oven to 425°F. Spread the apples in a 9 x 13-inch baking dish. Combine the butter, orange zest, cinnamon, salt, and pepper in a small bowl. Rinse the chicken and blot dry. Using poultry shears or a knife, cut the backbone out. Place the chicken split-side down on top of the apples. Rub half of the butter mixture underneath the skin. Rub the remaining half on the skin. Roast the chicken until the thickest part of the thigh reaches 180°F or the juices run clear when pricked, about 40 minutes. Tent the chicken to keep warm and let rest for about 5 minutes. Cut the chicken into pieces, and serve with the roasted apples and juices.

Yield: 4 servings *Prep Time:* 5 minutes *Cooking Time:* 40 minutes

CHICKEN WITH JALAPEÑO-CILANTRO SAUCE

Between the limey-cumin marinade that the chicken takes a soak in and the addition of a creamy Peruvian sauce spiked with jalapeño and cilantro, these chicken breasts are infused with flavor.

½ cup freshly squeezed lime juice

3½ tablespoons canola oil, divided

1½ teaspoons sweet paprika

2 teaspoons ground cumin

5 Whole Foods organic, free-range boneless chicken breasts (about 2½ pounds)

3 jalapeño chiles, seeded and coarsely chopped

1 cup loosely packed cilantro, coarsely chopped

1 clove garlic, crushed

⅓ cup low-fat mayonnaise

1 teaspoon freshly squeezed lime juice, plus more as needed

1 tablespoon water

kosher salt and freshly ground black pepper

Combine the lime juice, 2 tablespoons canola oil, paprika, and cumin in a small bowl. Put the chicken in a zippered bag, pour in the marinade, close securely, turn over and around to distribute the marinade, and put the bag in a bowl (in case of leakage). Refrigerate for 2 to 3 hours. Meanwhile, make the sauce: Add the chiles, cilantro, garlic, mayonnaise, lime juice, water, and ½ teaspoon salt to a food processor. Puree until smooth, 30 seconds to 1 minute. Taste and adjust the salt and lime juice as needed. Transfer to a container, and refrigerate until needed.

Preheat the oven to 400°F. Heat 1½ tablespoons canola oil in an ovenproof large sauté pan or skillet over high heat. Season the chicken with salt and pepper, and carefully add to the pan skin-side down. Cook the chicken until browned, about 8 minutes. Turn the chicken over, and cook another 2 minutes. Roast the chicken breasts to an internal temperature of 165°F, 15 to 20 minutes. Serve with the jalapeño-cilantro sauce.

Yield: 4 servings *Prep Time:* 15 minutes, plus 2 to 3 hours to marinate *Cooking Time:* 30 minutes

BRAISED CHIPOTLE TURKEY DRUMSTICKS WITH SWEET POTATOES

Pound per pound, turkey drumsticks are a lot cheaper than chicken. Like most cheaper meats, they do require a longer cooking time, but it's mostly unattended. Pair this with Couscous with Dried Cranberries and Pine Nuts (page 46) as an ode to Thanksgiving.

$

1 tablespoon canola oil

3 (1-pound) Whole Foods organic turkey drumsticks

kosher salt and freshly ground black pepper

1 medium yellow onion, chopped

4 cloves garlic, smashed

2 cups 365 Everyday Value Organic Chicken Broth

1 canned chipotle chile plus 2 teaspoons adobo sauce

3 medium sweet potatoes

1 tablespoon flour

1 tablespoon unsalted butter, at room temperature

Heat the canola oil in a large Dutch oven over medium-high heat. Season the drumsticks with salt. Brown for 3 to 4 minutes on each side. Transfer the drumsticks to a platter. Add the onion to the pot, stirring occasionally, cooking until slightly softened, 2 to 3 minutes. Add the garlic and cook 1 minute, then add the chicken broth, chipotle chile, adobo sauce, ½ teaspoon salt, and ¼ teaspoon pepper. Bring to a boil, then return the turkey to the pot. Cover with a lid, reduce the heat to low, and simmer for 1 hour. Meanwhile, peel the sweet potatoes, and chop into 1-inch dice. In a small bowl, combine the flour and the butter, and place in the freezer.

Turn the drumsticks over. Continue cooking, and after 40 minutes longer, add the sweet potatoes. Cook until the turkey and the sweet potatoes are very tender, about 20 minutes longer. Transfer the turkey and the sweet potatoes to a platter, and tent with foil to keep warm. Carefully remove the chile and all but 1½ cups of the broth from the pot. Turn the heat to high, whisk in the reserved butter and flour mixture, and boil until the sauce is the desired thickness, a few minutes. When the sauce is ready, pour over the turkey and sweet potatoes. To serve, use a fork to flake the turkey off the bone.

Yield: 4 servings *Prep Time:* 20 minutes *Cooking Time:* 2 hours

CHICKEN AND RICE WITH GINGER SAUCE

It sounds simple, but there's something intricately delicious about chicken and rice. Add a gingery sauce to pour over the chicken and stir into the rice, and magic happens. Serve this with Quick Sautéed Cucumbers with Crushed Red Pepper (page 44) for a totally Asian-inspired meal. Note: The knobbiness of the ginger makes it hard to use a peeler to remove the brown peel. An easier way is to use a spoon to scrape the peel away.

2 teaspoons plus ½ cup canola oil, divided

1½ pounds Whole Foods organic, free-range boneless, skinless chicken thighs

kosher salt

3 cups 365 Everyday Value Organic Chicken Broth or water

1½ cups uncooked basmati rice

½ pound fresh ginger, peeled and cut into 1-inch pieces

2 tablespoons water

Heat 2 teaspoons canola oil in a large heavy pot over high heat. Season the chicken thighs with salt and sauté just 2 to 3 minutes on each side, in batches if needed (browning isn't necessary). Transfer the chicken to a plate. Add the chicken broth or water to the pot, stirring to incorporate any bits on the bottom. Add the rice and ½ teaspoon salt, and bring to a boil. Return the chicken to the pot, and cover with lid. Reduce the heat to low, and simmer until the rice is tender, about 20 minutes. Remove from the heat and let sit 10 minutes.

Meanwhile, make the ginger sauce: In a food processor, puree the ginger, water, and ½ teaspoon salt while pouring ½ cup canola oil down the feed tube. Puree until emulsified. Taste the sauce, and adjust the seasoning as needed. Serve the chicken and rice with generous portions of ginger sauce.

Yield: 4 servings *Prep Time:* 10 minutes *Cooking Time:* 30 minutes

CHICKEN PARMESAN

This chicken Parmesan gets a healthy makeover, replacing the usual step for frying the breaded chicken cutlets with baking instead. So indulge in this creation without any guilt. Serve with Pesto-Stuffed Tomatoes (page 37).

2 pounds Whole Foods organic, free-range chicken cutlets

kosher salt and freshly ground black pepper

1 cup bread crumbs

1½ cups Whole Foods Grated Parmigiano-Reggiano cheese

3 eggs

extra-virgin olive oil, as needed

1 (4-ounce) ball Whole Foods fresh mozzarella, grated

1 (25-ounce) jar 365 Everyday Value Classic Organic Pasta Sauce

Preheat the oven to 400°F. Fit a wire rack on top of a rimmed baking sheet. To bread the chicken, season the cutlets with salt and pepper. In a medium bowl, combine the bread crumbs and Parmigiano-Reggiano cheese. In a small bowl, whisk the eggs until frothy. Dip each piece of chicken into the egg wash, letting the excess liquid drip off. Then, dredge both sides of the chicken in the bread crumb mixture. Place on the prepared wire rack. Repeat until all the chicken cutlets are coated. Drizzle the breaded chicken with olive oil, and bake until browned, 15 to 18 minutes. Using a spatula, transfer the cutlets to an ovenproof dish. Spread the mozzarella cheese and pasta sauce over the cutlets. Return to the oven, and bake the chicken until cooked through, 25 to 30 minutes. Serve.

Yield: 4 to 6 servings *Prep Time:* 15 minutes *Cooking Time:* 50 minutes

ORANGE-GLAZED CHICKEN OVER SPINACH

Orange marmalade does all the work for you, creating the sauce for this glazed chicken. Add a little spinach for a quick and healthy meal.

1 tablespoon canola oil, divided

1 (10-ounce) bag spinach

kosher salt and freshly ground black pepper

1½ pounds Whole Foods organic, free-range chicken cutlets

½ cup orange marmalade

2 tablespoons maple syrup

juice of 1 lemon

1 tablespoon low-sodium soy sauce

1 teaspoon poppy seeds

1 tablespoon almond slivers

Heat 1½ teaspoons canola oil in a large sauté pan or skillet over medium-high heat. Add half the spinach, and season with salt and pepper. Cook the spinach, stirring, until almost wilted, 2 to 3 minutes. Add the remaining spinach, and continue to cook, stirring again, until all the spinach is wilted, about 3 more minutes. Cover with the lid, remove from the heat, and set aside.

In a medium sauté pan or skillet, heat the remaining 1½ teaspoons canola oil over high heat. Season the chicken cutlets with salt and pepper, and add to the pan. Sauté until the chicken is golden, 2 to 3 minutes. Flip the chicken over and cook until golden, 2 to 3 minutes longer. Meanwhile, make the orange sauce: In a small bowl, whisk the orange marmalade, maple syrup, lemon juice, soy sauce, poppy seeds, and almonds until combined. When the chicken is golden, add the orange sauce to the chicken. Using tongs, coat the chicken with the sauce, letting the sauce reduce, until the chicken is well glazed, 2 to 3 minutes. Remove from the heat. Use a paper towel to blot any excess liquid from the reserved spinach. Divide the spinach among serving plates and top with the chicken. Pour the sauce over the chicken and serve.

Yield: 4 servings *Prep Time:* 5 minutes *Cooking Time:* 20 minutes

CHICKEN TENDERS WITH FRUIT SALSA

Chicken tenders get a makeover from a tangy fruit salsa. The produce at Whole Foods is always fresh, so you don't need to wait until summer to enjoy this dish. Low-Fat Creamed Spinach (page 39) makes this a complete meal.

2 Ruby Red grapefruits, segmented and cut into bite-size pieces (see page 95)

1 cup chopped pineapple (see sidebar)

1 mango, chopped (see page 26)

¼ cup sliced red onion

1 to 3 jalapeño chiles, seeded and chopped

¼ cup chopped cilantro

kosher salt and freshly ground black pepper

1½ pounds Whole Foods organic, free-range chicken breast tenders

2 teaspoons canola oil

Make the salsa: Supreme the grapefruits into a large bowl. Add the pineapple, mango, onion, jalapeño, cilantro, and ½ teaspoon salt, and stir to combine. Reserve. Season the chicken tenders with salt and pepper. Heat the canola oil in a medium sauté pan or skillet over medium-high heat. Working in batches if necessary, add the chicken and sauté until golden on one side, 2 to 3 minutes. Flip the chicken over and cook until golden, 2 to 3 minutes longer. Cut into the thickest piece to determine that it's no longer pink. Serve the chicken tenders with fruit salsa spooned over.

TO PEEL A PINEAPPLE:

Cut the stem from the pineapple. Stand the pineapple upright, and cut downward on all sides just deep enough to remove the peel. Use a paring knife to remove the "eyes" by making diagonal cuts across the flesh just deep enough to remove them. Then cut up the pineapple as needed.

Yield: 4 servings | *Prep Time:* 20 minutes | *Cooking Time:* 20 minutes

SCALLION-MARINATED CHICKEN

This scallion-heavy marinade pays homage to jerk flavors with a touch of allspice and thyme plus the heat of jalapeño.

$

2 bunches scallions, trimmed and coarsely chopped

2 jalapeño chiles, seeded and coarsely chopped

1½ tablespoons ground allspice

2 teaspoons dried thyme

4 cloves garlic

juice of 1 lime

1 tablespoon soy sauce

¼ cup plus 1 tablespoon canola oil, divided

1½ pounds Whole Foods organic, free-range boneless, skinless chicken thighs

kosher salt and freshly ground black peppers

In a food processor, add the scallions, jalapeños, allspice, thyme, garlic, lime juice, soy sauce, and ¼ cup canola oil. Puree until smooth, about 1 minute. Reserve ¼ cup of the marinade for basting. Pour the remaining marinade into a shallow dish, and add the chicken thighs. Cover and refrigerate 3 to 4 hours.

Preheat the oven to 400°F. Heat the remaining 1 tablespoon canola oil in a medium sauté pan or skillet over medium-high heat. Season the chicken thighs with salt and pepper, and cook until brown, about 5 minutes. Using tongs, flip the chicken thighs over and cook until brown, 4 to 5 minutes longer. Roast the chicken, occasionally basting with the remaining marinade, until a meat thermometer registers 180°F, 10 to 15 minutes. Serve.

Yield: 4 servings *Prep Time:* 15 minutes, plus 3 to 4 hours to marinate *Cooking Time:* 25 minutes

CHICKEN MARSALA

Marsala is a sweet, inexpensive fortified wine that lends a ton of flavor to any fare, especially its namesake dish, where chicken and vegetables are simmered in a Marsala-heavy broth. Serve this with Polenta with Dried Mushrooms (page 38). Note: The combination of equal amounts of butter and flour is called *beurre manié*, French for "kneaded butter." It's used as a quick and easy way to thicken any sauce.

2 teaspoons canola oil

1 (10-ounce) container white mushrooms, halved

1 pint cherry tomatoes

4 cloves garlic

1 cup 365 Everyday Value Organic Chicken Broth

¾ cup Marsala

kosher salt and freshly ground black pepper

2 pounds Whole Foods organic, free-range chicken cutlets

1 tablespoon unsalted butter, at room temperature

1 tablespoon flour

Heat the canola oil in a large sauté pan or skillet over medium-high heat. Sauté the mushrooms and tomatoes, stirring occasionally, until the mushrooms are golden, 2 to 3 minutes. Add the garlic, and cook 1 minute. Add the chicken broth, Marsala, ½ teaspoon salt, and ¼ teaspoon pepper, and use a spoon to scrape up any bits on the bottom. Bring the liquid to a boil. Season the chicken, then nestle into the liquid, spooning the mushrooms and tomatoes on top of the chicken. Cover with a lid, and reduce the heat to low. Simmer the chicken until cooked through, 20 to 25 minutes. Cut into the thickest chicken piece to check for doneness.

Meanwhile, mix the butter and the flour in a small bowl. Put in the freezer to harden. Transfer the chicken from the pan into a dish. Bring the liquid to a boil over high heat. Add the butter and flour mixture, and whisk until the sauce thickens, 1 to 2 minutes, until it's as thick as you want. Taste the sauce and adjust the seasonings as needed. Pour the sauce and vegetables over the chicken and serve.

Yield: 4 to 6 servings *Prep Time:* 15 minutes *Cooking Time:* 50 minutes

ASIAN-STYLE CHICKEN THIGHS

Creating a spice blend like the Asian one in this recipe and then rubbing it underneath the skin of the chicken thighs before they're sautéed is a simple way to add tons of flavor to a chicken dish.

2 tablespoons freshly grated fresh ginger

1 teaspoon ground cardamom

1 teaspoon ground cumin

grated zest of 2 limes plus 1 teaspoon juice

kosher salt and freshly ground black pepper

1½ tablespoons canola oil, divided

1½ pounds Whole Foods organic, free-range bone-in, skin-on chicken thighs

Preheat the oven to 400°F. Combine the ginger, cardamom, cumin, lime zest, lime juice, ½ teaspoon salt, and ½ tablespoon canola oil in a small bowl. Dividing the spice mixture evenly between the chicken pieces, use your fingers to lift the skin from the chicken, and rub the spice underneath. Make sure to wipe off any spice mixture that isn't under the skin because it will burn. Season the exterior of the chicken with salt and pepper. Heat the remaining 1 tablespoon canola oil in a medium nonstick sauté pan or skillet over medium-high heat. Add the chicken thighs, skin-side down, and leave untouched to brown, 6 to 8 minutes. Using tongs, flip each chicken thigh over. Cook until a meat thermometer registers 180°F, 10 to 15 minutes.

Yield: 4 servings *Prep Time:* 10 minutes *Cooking Time:* 25 minutes

MEAT

Many health-conscious eaters avoid beef and pork, but it's not necessary to totally eliminate anything from your diet. In moderation, all foods can be part of a healthy way of eating. While it's fun to go to the butcher counter and look over all those beautiful pink and red cuts of raw meat sitting there in all their glory, beware of the pitfalls when buying. Meat that has already been marinated or assembled (like kebabs or stuffed chops) comes at a much higher price tag. Don't fall for any of those traps—buy the meat, and prepare it for cooking yourself. Also, rely on cheaper cuts of meat. Chuck roast and veal shoulder turn into magic when cooked slowly over a longer period of time. If you splurge on the more expensive cuts, incorporate the meat into a dish with many other ingredients, like fajitas, to stretch the meat for more servings. Most of the dishes in this chapter are hearty and rewarding, providing you a meal you deserve after a long day of work, a meal you can enjoy with a glass of red wine or a beer.

BEEF FAJITAS WITH RED PEPPERS AND ONIONS

Sometimes we all get a hankering for steak. The best way to indulge in this craving without massive damage to the wallet is to incorporate this more expensive meat in a recipe like fajitas, where it's bulked up with veggies.

grated zest and juice of 2 limes
3 tablespoons olive oil
3 cloves garlic, smashed
1¼ teaspoons ground cumin
1½ pounds Whole Foods skirt steak
1 tablespoon canola oil
3 medium yellow onions, sliced
3 red bell peppers, sliced
kosher salt and freshly ground black pepper
¼ teaspoon cayenne pepper (optional)
1 package Whole Foods Whole Wheat Tortillas, warmed in the microwave, to serve
1 avocado, sliced (see page 8)

Combine the lime zest, lime juice, olive oil, garlic, and 1 teaspoon cumin in a shallow dish. Add the steak and turn over in the marinade to cover. Cover and refrigerate for 1 to 2 hours to marinate, no more (the acid in the lime juice will make the meat mushy).

Heat the canola oil in a large sauté pan or skillet over medium-high heat. Add the onion, and cook, stirring occasionally, just until translucent, about 5 minutes. Add the bell pepper, ½ teaspoon salt, the remaining ¼ teaspoon cumin, and cayenne and stir to combine. Cook, stirring occasionally, until the onions are mostly caramelized and the bell peppers are cooked, about 10 minutes longer. Taste and adjust the seasonings as needed. Keep hot.

Preheat the broiler. Line a rimmed baking sheet with foil. Remove the steak from the marinade and discard the marinade. Dab the steak with a paper towel to remove the marinade. Place on the prepared baking sheet and season with salt and pepper. Broil the steak about 4 minutes on each side, until it reaches medium-rare. Adjust the time for different thickness or doneness; if needed, make a cut into the center to determine doneness. Let the steak rest for 5 minutes, then cut across the grain into thin slices diagonally. Serve the steak and vegetables on the warmed tortillas with avocado slices.

Yield: 4 servings *Prep Time:* 15 minutes, plus 1 to 2 hours to marinate *Cooking Time:* 30 minutes

MEATLOAF

This meatloaf is still comfort-worthy even with a healthier spin using lean ground beef and an abundance of grated veggies. Find the brioche rolls in the Whole Foods bakery. This is just begging to be served with Buttermilk Mashed Potatoes (page 45).

$

2 brioche rolls, torn into small pieces

¼ cup milk

2 tablespoons 365 Everyday Value Organic Tomato Ketchup

2 teaspoons Worcestershire sauce

1 large zucchini, grated

1 large carrot, grated

1 large yellow squash, grated

1 clove garlic, minced

1 pound Whole Foods organic ground sirloin, 90 percent lean

1 egg

1 teaspoon kosher salt

½ teaspoon freshly ground black pepper

Preheat the oven to 350°F. Coat an 8 by 4-inch loaf pan with cooking spray. In a large bowl, combine the brioche and the milk, and let sit for 5 minutes. Squeeze the milk from the brioche, discarding the milk. Return the brioche to the bowl, and add the ketchup, Worcestershire sauce, zucchini, carrot, squash, garlic, beef, egg, salt, and pepper. Using a spoon or your hands, combine the meat mixture well, but do not overmix. Transfer to the prepared pan. Bake until the meatloaf is cooked through, 50 minutes to 1 hour.

Yield: 4 to 6 servings *Prep Time:* 20 minutes *Cooking Time:* 1 hour, unattended

BEEF TACOS

I always seem to have a lingering jar of salsa in my fridge and a container of sour cream with just a dollop left in it. That's when it's taco time—pick up some taco shells and ground beef, and use up all those leftover condiments. Also, I tend to pile on grated carrots or any other produce I want to get rid of. For toppings like shredded lettuce that you need only a small amount of, consider buying them from the Whole Foods salad bar.

1 tablespoon flour

1 tablespoon chili powder

1 teaspoon salt

1 teaspoon ground turmeric

½ teaspoon ground cumin

2 teaspoons canola oil

1 pound Whole Foods organic lean ground beef

¼ cup water

1 (5.5-ounce) package hard 365 Everyday Value Organic Blue Corn Taco Shells (12 shells)

Condiments:

6 to 8 radishes, chopped

2 tomatoes, chopped

1 cup shredded lettuce

salsa, as needed

Combine the flour, chili powder, salt, turmeric, and cumin in a small bowl. Heat the canola oil in a medium sauté pan or skillet over medium-high heat. Add the ground beef and sauté, stirring every couple of minutes to break up the meat, until the meat is browned and cooked, 6 to 7 minutes. Add the spice mixture and the water, and cook, stirring to coat the meat with the spices, until browned, 2 to 3 minutes. To serve, pile the meat into taco shells and let each guest add their own condiments.

Yield: 4 servings | *Prep Time:* 10 minutes | *Cooking Time:* 15 minutes

SKIRT STEAK IN LETTUCE WRAPS WITH PICKLED VEGETABLES

Lettuce serves as the wrap for broiled slices of skirt steak and quick-pickled veggies in this refreshing dish.

1 cup white vinegar
¼ cup sugar
1 bunch radishes, sliced
2 cucumbers, peeled and sliced
½ red onion, peeled and sliced
1¼ pounds Whole Foods skirt steak
kosher salt and freshly ground black pepper
2 heads Boston lettuce, leaves separated

Make the pickled vegetables: Whisk the vinegar and the sugar in a small bowl until the sugar is mostly dissolved. Add the radishes, cucumbers, and onion, submerging in the vinegar, and let sit 15 to 20 minutes.

Preheat the broiler. Line a rimmed baking sheet with foil, and place the steak on the baking sheet. Broil to the desired doneness, about 3 minutes per side. Transfer to a work surface, and cover with a piece of foil. Let the steak rest for 5 minutes, then slice thinly across the grain, diagonally. To serve, place the pickled vegetables, lettuce leaves, and steak on a platter. Let everyone assemble their own wraps by filling lettuce cups with meat and vegetables.

Yield: 4 servings *Prep Time:* 15 minutes *Cooking Time:* 15 minutes

BRAISED BEEF AND CABBAGE

Using beef cuts like chuck or bottom round is such a cheaper route to go in general and especially at Whole Foods. It takes a longer cooking time, yes, but it's all unattended and the resulting fork-tender meat is worth it. Also, veggies don't get much cheaper than a head of cabbage, making this a great budget-friendly meal.

$

1 tablespoon canola oil

kosher salt

1½ pounds Whole Foods extra lean beef chuck or bottom round, cut into 1½-inch cubes (see sidebar)

1 large head green cabbage, shredded

4 cloves garlic, coarsely chopped

1 cup 365 Everyday Value Organic Beef-Flavored Broth, divided

grated zest of ½ orange

1 tablespoon crème fraîche or sour cream

Heat the canola oil in a large heavy sauté pan or Dutch oven over medium-high heat. Season the beef with salt. Working in batches if needed, sear all sides of the meat, 2 to 3 minutes on each side. As the meat is browned, transfer to a plate. Still over medium-high heat, add half the cabbage. Sauté, stirring, until wilted, 2 to 4 minutes. Add the remaining cabbage and repeat. Stir in the garlic, cooking 30 seconds. Add ½ cup broth, stirring to get the tasty bits off the bottom of the pan. Add the remaining ½ cup broth and ½ teaspoon salt, and bring to a boil. Return the meat to the pot, cover with a lid, and reduce the heat to low so the liquid is simmering. Let simmer until the meat is fork tender, about 1½ hours. Taste and adjust the seasonings as needed. Remove from the heat, and stir in the orange zest and the crème fraîche. Serve.

TO CUT UP MEAT FOR STEW:

Pull the meat apart at the seams, and trim the fat. Examine the pieces of meat to figure out the best way to go about cutting. Then cut the meat into 1½-inch cubes. Don't be tempted to cut smaller cubes; you need hefty pieces to prevent drying out.

Yield: 4 servings | *Prep Time:* 10 minutes | *Cooking Time:* 2 hours

VEAL PAPRIKASH WITH EGG NOODLES

Avoid the cubed veal available at the butcher's counter; it could be tough if cut from the leg. Buy shoulder roast, and cut it up at home. For this recipe, it simmers in a paprika-flavored sauce that is served over egg noodles.

$

- 2 tablespoons canola oil
- 1½ pounds Whole Foods organic veal shoulder, cut into 1½ inch cubes (see page 90)
- kosher salt and freshly ground black pepper
- 1 onion, sliced
- 1 cup 365 Everyday Value Organic Chicken Broth
- 2 tablespoons sweet paprika
- 1 cup 365 Everyday Value Organic Low Fat Sour Cream
- 1 pound 365 Everyday Value Wide Enriched Egg Noodles

Heat the canola oil in a large heavy saucepan over medium-high heat. Season the veal with salt and pepper. Brown the veal on each side, 2 to 3 minutes per side. Add the onion slices, and cook, stirring, until translucent, 2 to 3 minutes. Add the broth and the paprika, and stir to combine. Bring the liquid to a boil, cover with a lid, then reduce the heat to low. Simmer until the meat is tender, about 45 minutes. Remove from the heat and stir in the sour cream. Season to taste.

Meanwhile, cook the noodles in large pot of boiling salted water until tender but still firm to the bite, stirring occasionally. Drain the noodles, and transfer to serving plates. Spoon the veal and the sauce over the noodles and serve.

Yield: 4 servings *Prep Time:* 5 minutes *Cooking Time:* 55 minutes

BANGERS AND ONION GRAVY OVER POTATOES

This is a spin on Irish cuisine, serving Irish bangers in an onion gravy over split baked potatoes. I'm a Southern gal, so this reminds me of the biscuits and gravy I grew up on.

$

4 medium russet potatoes

4 Whole Foods Irish bangers

1 tablespoon canola oil

2 large sweet onions, chopped

½ teaspoon kosher salt

1½ tablespoons flour

1 cup 365 Everyday Value Organic Beef-Flavored Broth, divided

⅓ cup milk

Preheat the oven to 400°F. Using a fork or knife, poke numerous holes into the potatoes. Place on the middle rack. Bake until a knife inserted into a potato slides in easily, 60 to 75 minutes.

Meanwhile, make the bangers and onion gravy. Poke holes in the bangers. Fill a medium pot with water and bring to a boil over high heat. Cook the bangers until no longer pink in the center, about 15 to 18 minutes. Remove from the water, and when cool enough to handle, chop the bangers into pieces. Heat the canola oil in a large sauté pan or skillet over medium-high heat. Sauté the onions, stirring occasionally, just until translucent, about 5 minutes. Reduce the heat to medium, and cook until the onions are mostly caramelized, about 20 minutes longer. Add the salt and the flour, and stir to combine with the onions. Carefully add ½ cup beef broth, stirring constantly, until thickened. Add the remaining broth and the milk, and continue to cook until as thick as you like. Add the banger pieces, and stir to combine. Season to taste. Split each baked potato open lengthwise, and fill with the bangers and onion gravy. Serve.

Yield: 4 servings *Prep Time:* 10 minutes *Cooking Time:* 75 minutes, mostly unattended

PORK SPARERIBS WITH HOISIN SAUCE

Hoisin sauce is a pungent Chinese barbecue sauce. These spareribs are delicious served with sautéed spinach and white rice studded with scallions. For a truly meat-and-potatoes meal, serve these with Smashed "Fried" Potatoes (page 48).

$

4 pounds Whole Foods pork spareribs

kosher salt and freshly ground black pepper

2 tablespoons canola oil

½ cup plus 3 tablespoons hoisin sauce, divided

⅔ cup soy sauce

½ cup Marsala

¼ cup rice vinegar

1 tablespoon honey

Using poultry shears, cut the spareribs into pieces about 4-inches long. Season with salt and pepper. Heat the canola oil in a large heavy sauté pan or Dutch oven over high heat. In batches, brown the ribs, 3 to 4 minutes per side. Transfer to a plate. Discard the oil, and add ½ cup hoisin sauce, soy sauce, Marsala, and rice vinegar to the pan. Over medium-high heat, bring liquid to a boil, and add the browned ribs. Cover with a lid, reduce to low, and simmer, turning halfway through, until the ribs are slightly tender, about 45 minutes. Remove from the heat.

Preheat the broiler. Line a rimmed baking sheet with foil. Combine the remaining 3 tablespoons hoisin sauce and the honey in a small bowl. Transfer the ribs from the pan to the prepared baking sheet. Brush the hoisin and honey glaze on the ribs. Broil the ribs until the glaze is fused onto the ribs, 2 to 3 minutes. Add more glaze, if desired, and serve.

Yield: 4 servings | *Prep Time:* 15 minutes | *Cooking Time:* 1 hour unattended

PORK TENDERLOIN WITH ORANGE AND FENNEL RELISH

The trick to cooking pork tenderloin is to remove it from the oven at the correct internal temperature before it overcooks. Also, if you're not comfortable supreming the oranges, substitute with 2 (11-ounce) cans of drained mandarin oranges. For the olives in the relish, I prefer the oil-cured from Whole Foods salad bar.

4 oranges, segmented (see sidebar)

3 large fennel bulbs, trimmed of feathery stalks and chopped

½ cup coarsely chopped parsley

½ cup pitted black olives, coarsely chopped

1½ tablespoons extra-virgin olive oil

kosher salt and freshly ground black pepper

1 (1-pound) Whole Foods pork tenderloin

2 teaspoons canola oil

Preheat the oven to 400°F. Make the orange and fennel relish: Supreme the oranges (see sidebar) into a bowl. Add the fennel, parsley, and olives. Stir to combine, and drizzle with the olive oil. Season with salt and pepper and set aside.

Season the pork tenderloin with salt and pepper. Heat the canola oil in a sauté pan or skillet over high heat. Sauté the pork on each side until golden brown, 2 to 3 minutes per side. Roast the pork until a meat thermometer registers 145°F, about 10 minutes. Remove from the oven, and let rest for 10 minutes. Thinly slice the pork diagonally. Serve with the orange and fennel relish.

TO SUPREME CITRUS FRUIT:

Use a serrated knife to slice off about ½ inch from the bottom and the top of the fruit. Place the fruit bottom-down on a work surface, and use the serrated knife to remove the peel and pith from the entire fruit. Over a bowl to catch the juice, use a paring knife to cut each segment from between the two membranes, dropping the segment into the bowl.

Yield: 4 servings | *Prep Time:* 15 minutes | *Cooking Time:* 10 minutes

POLENTA CASSEROLE WITH PORK CHOPS

Polenta and pork chops are both cheap ingredients that are transformed into a tasty casserole.

$

1 pound Whole Foods center-cut boneless pork chops

1 teaspoon kosher salt, divided

¼ teaspoon freshly ground black pepper

½ teaspoon dried thyme

2 teaspoons canola oil

1 (15-ounce) jar 365 Everyday Value Part Skim Milk Ricotta Cheese

1 (7-ounce) jar 365 Everyday Value Basil Pesto

½ cup Whole Foods Grated Parmigiano-Reggiano cheese

1 egg, beaten

4 cups skim milk, plus more as needed

1½ cups coarse cornmeal

Preheat the oven to 350°F. Season the pork chops with ½ teaspoon salt, pepper, and thyme. Heat the canola oil in a medium sauté pan or skillet over medium-high heat. Quickly sauté the pork chops, just 2 minutes on each side. Remove the pork chops from the pan, and reserve. Combine the ricotta cheese, pesto, Parmigiano-Reggiano cheese, and egg in a bowl. Reserve. Coat a 9 x 13-inch rectangular baking dish with cooking spray; set aside. In a medium pot, bring the milk and remaining ½ teaspoon salt to a simmer over medium-high heat. Lower the heat to medium-low, and pour the cornmeal into the milk, while vigorously whisking. Cook, stirring constantly, until the polenta is thick, 3 to 5 minutes. Remove from the heat.

Pour half of the polenta into the prepared baking dish, using a spatula to spread the polenta into an even layer. Working quickly, spread half of the ricotta mixture on top of the polenta. Add the pork chops, followed by another layer of the remaining ricotta mixture. Top with the remaining polenta. If the polenta has gotten too thick, return to the stove over medium heat, add more milk, and whisk until the polenta is soft again. Bake, uncovered, until the casserole is heated through and the top is lightly golden, about 15 minutes.

Yield: 4 servings *Prep Time:* 20 minutes *Cooking Time:* 15 minutes

SHEPHERD'S PIE

This lightened-up version of shepherd's pie has pureed cauliflower standing in for the traditional mashed potatoes.

$

1 teaspoon kosher salt, divided

1 (1-pound) head cauliflower, chopped

½ cup milk

2 teaspoons canola oil

1 pound Whole Foods ground lamb

2 cloves garlic, minced

½ (16-ounce) package frozen 365 Everyday Value Organic Green Peas, thawed

Preheat the oven to 350°F. Bring a large pot of salted water to a boil over high heat. Cook the cauliflower until tender, about 8 minutes, depending on size of the cauliflower florets. Drain the cauliflower in a colander. Puree the cauliflower with the milk and ½ teaspoon salt in a food processor or blender, until smooth. Set aside.

Heat the canola oil in a medium sauté pan or skillet over medium-high heat. Add the lamb and the remaining ½ teaspoon salt. Sauté, stirring occasionally to break up the meat, until browned, 5 to 7 minutes. Add the garlic and the peas, and cook 2 minutes longer, stirring constantly. Remove from the heat, and drain any remaining oil from the lamb. Transfer the mixture to an ovenproof 9 x 13-inch casserole dish. Spread the cauliflower over the top. Bake, uncovered, until the top is golden and the casserole is hot throughout, 20 to 25 minutes. Serve.

Yield: 4 servings *Prep Time:* 30 minutes *Cooking Time:* 30 minutes

FISH & SHELLFISH

Seafood has a lot of benefits for your health and can feel like a luxury. Unfortunately, it can also be very expensive. Never fear—with a few tricks up your sleeve, there are ways to add seafood to your diet and deliciousness to your dinner plate without blowing a hole through your food budget. First off, you can focus on more-affordable fish, like catfish and tilapia. You should also keep an eye out for sales; the seafood prices at Whole Foods can be a little steep, but they often have good weekly sale prices. Also, stock up on the Whole Foods line of frozen fish and shellfish, which is high quality but more budget friendly than what's offered at the fish counter. Another alternative is to buy smaller quantities of the pricey stuff and augment the dish with other protein-rich ingredients, like meats and beans. And finally, sometimes it's simply worth splurging and finding other ways to cut down on your food budget.

MUSSELS WITH COCONUT MILK AND LEMONGRASS

Most mussel instructions say to soak in water extensively and trim the beard with scissors. However, most farm-raised mussels, including those from Whole Foods, come pretty darn clean, but they still need a quick soak in a bowl of water. To use lemongrass, smash it with a knife, remove the outer layers, and chop the small inner layer that's full of flavor.

1 teaspoon canola oil

1 stalk lemongrass, chopped (see note)

2 cloves garlic, minced

1-inch piece fresh ginger, grated

1 jalapeño chile, seeded and finely chopped

1 cup light coconut milk

2 pounds Whole Foods farm-raised cultured mussels, scrubbed and debearded

2 tablespoons chopped cilantro

1 tablespoon unsalted butter

Whole Foods French bread, as needed

Heat the canola oil in a large heavy pot over medium-high heat. Add the lemongrass, garlic, ginger, and jalapeño. Cook, stirring constantly, until fragrant, 30 seconds to 1 minute. Add the coconut milk and increase the heat to high. Once the liquid reaches a boil, add the mussels and cover with a lid. Cook until most of the mussels are open, 4 to 5 minutes. Discard any unopened mussels. Transfer the mussels into two large bowls, leaving the broth in the pan. Place the pan over high heat, and add the cilantro and the butter. Boil the broth until reduced to the thickness you like, 2 to 3 minutes, then pour over the mussels. Serve with bread to dip in the broth.

Yield: 2 servings *Prep Time:* 10 minutes *Cooking Time:* 7 minutes

SALMON WITH HONEY GLAZE

The salmon in the Whole Foods frozen section is a few bucks cheaper per pound than from the fish counter, so that's my choice for this Asian-inspired dish. Serve with Whole Foods forbidden rice (also called black rice) for a healthy, simple meal.

⅓ cup soy sauce

1 tablespoon freshly squeezed lemon juice

1 tablespoon mustard

2 teaspoons grated fresh ginger

2 fillets Whole Foods frozen salmon, thawed (¾ pound)

1 teaspoon honey

In a small, shallow bowl, whisk the soy sauce, mustard, lemon juice, and ginger until combined. Pat the salmon fillets dry with paper towels and put in the marinade skin-side up. Cover and refrigerate for 20 minutes. Preheat the broiler. Line a rimmed baking sheet with foil. Remove the salmon from the marinade and pat dry. Place the salmon skin-side down on the prepared baking sheet. Drizzle the salmon with the honey. Broil 3 to 4 minutes, then rotate the baking sheet, and cook until desired doneness in center, 3 to 4 minutes longer. Serve.

Yield: 2 servings *Prep Time:* 5 minutes, plus time to refrigerate *Cooking Time:* 6 to 8 minutes

MOJO-MARINATED SHRIMP KEBABS

Mojo is the name of a Cuban sauce made from sour oranges, but the taste can be replicated with a combination of orange juice and lime juice. Just a dip in a citrus marinade delivers flavor for the shrimp. Try serving with Roasted Brussels Sprouts with Mustard Seeds (page 43), which balances well with the lightness of the shrimp.

grated zest of 1 orange plus juice of 3 oranges
grated zest of 1 lime plus juice of 5 limes
3 cloves garlic, minced
1 tablespoon chili powder
1½ teaspoons ground cumin
1 teaspoon dried oregano
1½ pounds Whole Foods farm-raised medium shrimp, peeled and deveined
2 tablespoons unsalted butter, melted
grated zest and juice of 1 lemon
2 teaspoons hot sauce

Soak 20 to 25 (6-inch) wooden skewers in water for 30 minutes. In a shallow dish, combine the orange juice, lime juice, garlic, chili powder, cumin, and oregano. Add the shrimp, stir to coat with the marinade, cover, and refrigerate for 30 to 45 minutes. Preheat the broiler. Remove the shrimp from the marinade. Thread the skewers with 4 to 5 shrimps each, and place on a rimmed baking sheet. Mix the melted butter with the lemon zest and juice and the hot sauce in a small bowl. Brush the shrimp with the sauce. Broil the shrimp until cooked through and pink, 2 to 3 minutes.

Yield: 4 servings *Prep Time:* 10 minutes, plus time to marinate *Cooking Time:* 6 minutes

BLACKENED CATFISH TACOS

At around $9.99 a pound, catfish is one of the cheapest fish options from Whole Foods. Blackened catfish is a classic Cajun dish using bold seasoning that works well in a taco.

$

2 tablespoons low-fat mayonnaise

1 tablespoon 365 Everyday Value Organic Apple Cider Vinegar, or more as needed

kosher salt and freshly ground black pepper

⅓ large green cabbage, thinly sliced

2 carrots, shredded using box grater

1½ pounds Whole Foods freshwater farm-raised catfish fillets

1½ tablespoons 365 Everyday Value Blackened Cajun Spice seasoning

8 (6-inch) Whole Foods Whole Wheat Tortillas, warmed in microwave

Preheat the oven to 400°F. Line a rimmed baking sheet with foil. Make the slaw: Combine the mayonnaise, vinegar, and ¼ teaspoon salt in a medium bowl. Stir in the cabbage and the carrots. Taste and adjust the vinegar and salt, as needed. Cut the catfish into 1-inch strips, and season both sides with Cajun spice, salt, and pepper. Transfer the catfish to the prepared baking sheet. Bake until the catfish is cooked, 10 to 12 minutes. Spread the tortillas on another baking sheet and warm in the oven while the catfish is cooking. To serve, layer catfish pieces onto each tortilla. Top with slaw and serve.

Yield: 4 servings, 8 tacos *Prep Time:* 15 minutes *Cooking Time:* 10 to 12 minutes

LOW COUNTRY BOIL

Low country boils are an institution in parts of the South. To make it more affordable, this recipe has zucchini and artichokes standing in for the more expensive seafood normally used in a boil. I love crawfish and was happy to discover that Whole Foods sells it already cooked for a very reasonable price.

$

¼ cup 365 Everyday Value Blackened Cajun Spice seasoning

2 medium artichokes

4 to 6 medium red potatoes, halved

4 uncooked Whole Foods chicken sausages

4 ears fresh corn, halved

2 zucchini, cut in half across, then lengthwise

½ pound cooked crawfish

melted butter, as needed

1 lemon, quartered, for garnish

Add the Cajun spice to a six-quart pot of water and bring to a boil over high heat. Meanwhile, prepare the artichokes: cut a half inch off the top and cut off the stem. Then cut the artichokes in half, from top to bottom. (This way, you can remove the choke and they will cook faster and be neater to eat.) When the water is boiling, add the artichokes, and cook for 20 minutes. Add the potatoes and the sausage, and cook for 20 minutes longer. Add the corn and the zucchini, and cook until the corn is bright yellow, about 3 minutes. Add the crawfish, and cook for 1 to 2 minutes. Remove the boil from the heat and drain in a colander. Serve with melted butter for the artichokes, and garnish with lemon wedges.

Yield: 4 servings | *Prep Time:* 10 minutes | *Cooking Time:* 45 minutes

WHOLE TROUT WITH ROASTED GARLIC AND PRESERVED LEMON

This baked whole trout is easy to make with two convenient shortcuts. Preserved lemons give a puck of saltiness and tartness, all in one shot. They can take a month to preserve on your own, or you can just pluck them from the shelf at the Whole Foods prepared food aisle. The roasted garlic is found in the Whole Foods olive bar. If they're out of roasted garlic, substitute 4 fresh cloves chopped garlic.

3 tablespoons unsalted butter, cut into pieces, at room temperature

⅓ cup chopped parsley

grated zest and juice of 1 lemon

½ teaspoon kosher salt

¼ teaspoon freshly ground black pepper

25 cloves roasted garlic from the Whole Foods olive bar

4 (¾-pound) whole trout

4 slices Whole Foods preserved lemon

1½ tablespoons olive oil

Preheat the oven to 350°F. Combine the butter, parsley, lemon zest, lemon juice, salt, and pepper in a small bowl. On a work surface, chop the garlic, then use the side of the knife to mash the garlic into a paste-like consistency. Mix the paste into the butter mixture with a spoon. Line a rimmed baking sheet with foil and coat with cooking spray. Open each trout, and season with salt and pepper. Stuff each trout with one-fourth of the butter mixture and 1 slice preserved lemon, and place on the prepared baking sheet. Drizzle the olive oil over the fish. Bake the trout until their flesh is flaky, about 30 minutes. Remove from the oven, and serve.

Yield: 4 servings | *Prep Time:* 10 minutes | *Cooking Time:* 30 minutes

WHITE BEANS, PESTO, AND SHRIMP

Tender cannellini beans have a very neutral flavor, which allows them to add a little heft to this dish without distracting from the flavor of the shrimp and the pesto.

2 (15-ounce) cans 365 Everyday Value Cannellini Beans, rinsed and drained

¾ cup fresh Whole Foods Pesto

1 tablespoon extra-virgin olive oil

1½ pounds Whole Foods farm-raised medium shrimp, peeled and deveined

kosher salt and freshly ground black pepper

juice of 1 lemon

Combine the beans and pesto thoroughly in a large bowl. Heat the olive oil in a large skillet over high heat. Sauté the shrimp until pink, 2 to 3 minutes. Remove from the heat and season with salt, pepper, and lemon juice. Divide the pesto beans among serving bowls and stir gently to combine. Top with the shrimp, and serve.

Yield: 4 servings *Prep Time:* 5 to 10 minutes *Cook Time:* 3 minutes

TILAPIA FISH CAKES WITH CAPER TARTAR SAUCE

Tilapia is one of the most budget-friendly fish out there, and with its mild flavor, it can be used in numerous recipes. For these fish cakes, the tarter sauce is both incorporated into the fish cakes and then served alongside. Serve with Cilantro Brown Rice (page 54).

- 1½ pounds Whole Foods tilapia
- kosher salt and freshly ground black pepper
- extra-virgin olive oil
- 1 cup low-fat mayonnaise
- 2 tablespoons 365 Everyday Value Capers, chopped
- juice of 1½ lemons
- 1½ tablespoons sweet pickle relish
- 1 egg
- 2½ cups panko bread crumbs, or more as needed
- canola oil

Preheat the oven to 425°F. Line a rimmed baking sheet with foil. Add the tilapia to the baking sheet, season with salt and pepper, and drizzle with olive oil. Bake the fish until it can be flaked with a fork, 10 to 12 minutes. Remove from the oven, transfer to another baking sheet, and let cool.

Meanwhile, make the tartar sauce: Combine the mayo, capers, one-third of the lemon juice, and the pickle relish in a large bowl. Transfer half the tartar sauce to a small container, and refrigerate until needed. Transfer the fish to the large bowl. Using a fork, flake the fish into pieces. Add the remaining lemon juice, egg, ½ cup bread crumbs, ½ teaspoon salt, and ¼ teaspoon pepper, and stir to combine the ingredients. Divide the fish mixture into 8 equal portions to form the cakes.

Coat a large nonstick sauté pan or skillet with canola oil, and heat over medium-high heat. Spread 2 cups bread crumbs in a shallow dish. Working in batches, dip the fish cakes into the bread crumbs to coat, and cook on each side until browned, just a few minutes. Transfer to a paper towel–lined plate. Serve with the remaining tartar sauce.

Yield: 8 fish cakes | *Prep Time:* 15 minutes | *Cooking Time:* 25 minutes

TUNA-STUFFED RED BELL PEPPERS

Stuffing red bell peppers with tuna salad creates a light, no-cook meal option. Find the roasted red bell peppers either in the olive bar or the prepared food aisle at Whole Foods. Also, such a small amount of olives are used that if you don't have any already in your fridge, just get them from the olive bar, too.

3 tablespoons low-fat mayonnaise
2 teaspoons freshly squeezed lemon juice
kosher salt and freshly ground black pepper
2 tablespoons chopped green olives
2 (6-ounce) cans 365 Everyday Value Albacore Tuna in Spring Water, drained
2 stalks celery, chopped
1 carrot, grated
1 cucumber, peeled and chopped
4 Whole Foods whole roasted red bell peppers

Combine the mayonnaise, lemon juice, ½ teaspoon salt, ¼ teaspoon pepper, and olives. Add the tuna, celery, carrot, and cucumber. Use a fork to combine the tuna with the vegetables. Taste and adjust the seasonings as needed. Cut each of the peppers down the center, then fill equally with the tuna salad. Serve.

Yield: 4 servings *Prep Time:* 15 minutes

VEGETARIAN

Even for meat eaters, it's nice to have a vegetarian meal every so often. There are plenty of ways to get protein without eating meat, and you'll feel good about your choice for health and ethical reasons. Now I'm a total carnivore, but even I choose to have a break for a variety of reasons. Not only is it a healthier option, it's usually a cheaper route to go. Sources of protein like quinoa, edamame, or beans are a ton less-expensive than their meat counterparts. An array of veggies incorporated into your diet also adds a slew of nutrients and vitamins. It's win-win.

PITAS WITH BAKED FALAFEL AND CUCUMBER-YOGURT SAUCE

Baking the falafel makes them a lot healthier than the traditional fried variety. With the delicious sauce, you'll barely notice the taste difference. The roasted garlic can be found at Whole Foods olive bar. If unavailable, substitute 2 cloves fresh garlic.

For the falafel:

2 (15-ounce) cans 365 Everyday Value Organic Garbanzo Beans, rinsed and drained

10 to 12 cloves roasted garlic from the Whole Foods olive bar

juice of ½ lemon

3 tablespoons flour

½ teaspoon baking powder

½ teaspoon kosher salt

1 teaspoon ground coriander

½ teaspoon red pepper flakes

1 egg

For the cucumber-yogurt sauce:

5 cloves roasted garlic from the Whole Foods olive bar

1 cup nonfat Fage Greek yogurt

1 tablespoon freshly squeezed lemon juice

2 tablespoons finely diced cucumber

¼ teaspoon kosher salt

To serve:

6 to 8 pita breads, warmed in the microwave

2 carrots, grated

sliced tomatoes

Make the falafel: Preheat the oven to 425°F. Line a rimmed baking sheet with foil and coat with cooking spray. Add the chickpeas, garlic, lemon juice, flour, baking powder, salt, coriander, pepper flakes, and egg to a food processor. Process just 30 seconds to 1 minute until somewhat pureed but still chunky. Form the falafel mixture into balls about the size of a golf ball, placing on the prepared baking sheet. Bake until slightly crisped on the outside, about 30 minutes. Meanwhile, make the cucumber-yogurt sauce: Mince the roasted garlic, then use the side of the knife to make a paste of the garlic. Combine the roasted garlic, yogurt, lemon juice, cucumber, and salt in a small bowl. Taste to adjust the seasonings as needed.

To serve, place cooked falafel in the pocket of a pita. Garnish with the sauce, grated carrots, and tomato slices.

Yield: 6 to 8 pita sandwiches *Prep Time:* 5 minutes *Cooking Time:* 15 minutes

SCALLION QUINOA WITH CORN AND SQUASH

Quinoa is a grain-like seed crop native to the Andes. It's a complete protein source and a good source of fiber, so it's a much healthier alternative to pasta salads for potlucks and cookouts. Serve this versatile dish at any temperature and feel free to add any vegetables you like.

1½ cups quinoa

3 cups water

kosher salt

1½ cups 2% Fage Greek yogurt

1 tablespoon freshly squeezed lime juice

3 scallions, green parts only, coarsely chopped

1½ tablespoons soy sauce

1 tablespoon unsalted butter

2 yellow squash, finely diced

2 cups fresh or frozen corn kernels (about 4 ears corn)

1 cup chopped bok choy

4 ounces goat cheese, crumbled

Add the quinoa, water, and ½ teaspoon salt to a medium pot. Bring to a boil over high heat, cover, reduce the heat to low, and simmer until tender, about 15 minutes. Remove from the heat. Meanwhile, puree the yogurt, lime juice, scallions, and soy sauce in a food processor until smooth, about 1 minute. Reserve. Melt the butter in a sauté pan or skillet over medium-high heat. Add the squash, and sauté 2 to 3 minutes. Add the corn and the boy choy and sauté, stirring, until the bok choy is wilted, 2 to 3 minutes longer. Transfer the quinoa to a large serving bowl. Add the yogurt mixture, and stir to combine. Then, add the vegetables and mix. Top with the cheese and serve.

Yield: 4 servings *Prep Time:* 15 minutes *Cooking Time:* 25 minutes

BLACK BEAN BURGERS

I'm a total carnivore, but these black bean burgers make me very happy. It's a healthier option than a meat burger and packed with nutrition to boot. Also, feel free to play around with the recipe, substituting different grains, nuts, and beans.

1¼ cups canned 365 Everyday Value Organic Black Beans, rinsed and drained

1 cup 365 frozen Organic Whole Grain Brown Rice, thawed

¾ cup cashews

1 tablespoon soy sauce

¼ cup parsley sprigs

1 egg

½ teaspoon kosher salt

¼ teaspoon freshly ground black pepper

2 tablespoon canola oil

4 to 5 hamburger buns, to serve

lettuce leaves and tomato slices, to serve

Add the black beans, brown rice, cashews, soy sauce, parsley, egg, salt, and pepper to a food processor. Pulse the mixture until smooth, about 1 minute. Form into 4 to 5 patties. Heat the canola oil in a medium nonstick sauté pan or skillet over medium-high heat. Carefully add the patties (they are fragile), and cook until slightly browned on each side, 2 to 3 minutes on each side. Serve on the buns with lettuce and tomatoes, and the desired condiments.

Yield: 4 servings *Prep Time:* 5 minutes *Cooking Time:* 10 minutes

OVEN-BAKED HASH BROWNS WITH EGGS

I'll be honest—these oven-baked hash browns aren't as pretty as their fried counterpart, but they're just as tasty and a heck of a lot healthier. Served with fried eggs, hash browns are turned into a meal.

- 4 medium to large russet potatoes (1½ to 2 pounds)
- 2 teaspoons freshly squeezed lemon juice
- 1 teaspoon kosher salt
- ¼ teaspoon freshly ground black pepper
- 2½ tablespoons olive oil, divided
- 4 eggs

Preheat the oven to 400°F. Line a rimmed baking sheet with foil. Position a box grater in a large bowl, and grate the potatoes. Using 1 or 2 paper towels, gently squeeze the potatoes, blotting the excess moisture. Add the lemon juice, salt, and pepper, and stir to combine. Using a tablespoon, drop small mounds of potatoes onto the prepared baking sheet, flattening each one. Drizzle the potatoes with 2 tablespoons olive oil. Bake until crisped around the edges, 40 to 50 minutes. Remove from the oven. Meanwhile, in a large nonstick skillet, heat ½ tablespoon olive oil over medium-high heat. Crack the eggs into the pan, and cook until the egg whites set, 1 to 2 minutes. Flip the eggs, and cook the yolks just briefly, about 30 seconds to 1 minute. Remove from the heat. To serve, divide the hash browns among serving plates and top each with an egg.

Yield: 4 servings *Prep Time:* 5 minutes *Cooking time:* 50 minutes, mostly unattended

CHILAQUILES

This spin on a traditional Mexican dish can be eaten any time of day. The tortilla chips soak up all the flavor of the salsa, making this superfast dish taste like it was slow-cooked.

1 cup smooth-style salsa, like 365 Everyday Value Organic Medium Salsa

1 (16-ounce) bag tortilla chips, slightly broken

1 (15-ounce) can 365 Everyday Value Organic Refried Black Beans

4 eggs

2 scallions, chopped

Heat the salsa and chips in a large nonstick skillet over medium-high heat. Cook, stirring, until the chips are soft from absorbing the sauce, 3 to 4 minutes. Meanwhile, spread the refried beans in a microwave-safe dish and heat in the microwave until hot, 3 to 4 minutes. Divide the beans among 4 plates, and layer the chips on top, adding any salsa not absorbed. Wipe out the pan, coat with cooking spray, and heat over medium-high heat. Crack the eggs into the pan, and cook until the egg whites are set, 3 to 4 minutes. Remove from the heat. Top each plate with an egg and garnish with scallions. Serve.

Yield: 4 servings | *Prep Time:* 5 minutes | *Cooking time:* 10 minutes

ROSEMARY FOCACCIA WITH ROASTED YELLOW TOMATOES

Made from Whole Foods whole wheat pizza dough, this focaccia offers a healthier twist on the classic. The yellow tomatoes can be found in the Whole Foods prepared food aisle and artichoke hearts and piquillo peppers in the salad bar.

flour, as needed

1 ball Whole Foods whole wheat pizza dough, at room temperature

2 tablespoons olive oil, divided

3 sprigs rosemary, leaves removed

¾ teaspoon kosher salt

1 red onion, sliced

⅓ pound Whole Foods roasted yellow tomatoes

⅓ pound artichoke hearts and piquillo peppers from the Whole Foods salad bar

Preheat the oven to 425°F. Sprinkle 1 to 2 tablespoons flour onto a work surface. Place the pizza dough on the work surface and gently knead and stretch the dough. Drizzle an 8 by 12-inch glass baking dish with 1 tablespoon olive oil and spread the pizza dough in the dish, pressing the dough down into the bottom of the dish. Use your fingers to punch tiny indentations into the top of the dough. Press rosemary leaves into the dough, and sprinkle with salt. Layer the onion, tomatoes, artichokes, and peppers on the dough. Bake until the focaccia is puffy and golden, 25 to 30 minutes. Drizzle with the remaining 1 tablespoon olive oil and cut into pieces.

Yield: 4 servings | *Prep Time:* 10 minutes | *Cooking Time:* 30 minutes

TWICE-BAKED SWEET POTATOES

Twice-baked potatoes are always a crowd-pleaser. A little honey helps highlight these creamy and delicious sweet potatoes.

4 medium sweet potatoes
1½ tablespoons unsalted butter
2 tablespoons soy sauce
1 tablespoon honey
2 tablespoons heavy cream
2 teaspoons Sriracha, or similar hot sauce

Preheat the oven to 425°F. Line a rimmed baking sheet with foil. Using a fork, poke holes in the sweet potatoes and place on the prepared baking sheet. Bake until a knife can be easily inserted into a potato, about 1 hour. Remove from the oven and let rest until cool enough to handle, 10 to 15 minutes. Increase the oven temperature to 450°F. Cut each sweet potato in half lengthwise, and scoop the flesh into a bowl. Add the butter, soy sauce, honey, cream, and hot sauce, and stir to combine. Spoon the sweet potato mixture into the skins. Return to the baking sheet and bake until hot, 10 to 15 minutes. Serve.

Yield: 2 to 4 servings *Prep Time:* 5 minutes *Cook Time:* 75 minutes

FLATBREAD WITH CARROT PUREE AND MARINATED GOAT CHEESE

You can do a lot of great things with a ball of pizza dough. The goat cheese adds a lot, but the real star here is the carrot puree. Eating this dish will be a startling reminder of just how flavorful some simple carrots can be.

2 teaspoons canola oil

1 cup chopped yellow onion

1 pound carrots, chopped (about 8 to 10)

1 to 1½ cups water

kosher salt and freshly ground black pepper

1 tablespoon unsalted butter

flour, as needed

1 ball Whole Foods pizza dough, at room temperature

¼ pound Whole Foods Marinated Goat Cheese, crumbled, marinade reserved

Position a rack in the middle of the oven and preheat the oven to 450°F. Heat the canola oil in a large sauté pan or skillet over medium-high heat. Add the onion, and cook until translucent, 2 to 3 minutes. Add the carrots and 1 cup water. Cook until the carrots are tender, about 10 minutes. If the water has evaporated, add the remaining ½ cup water. Remove from the heat, and season to taste with salt and pepper. Transfer the carrots to a food processor, add the butter, and puree until smooth, 1 to 2 minutes. Taste and adjust the seasoning as needed.

Dust a work surface and your hands with 1 to 2 tablespoons flour. Remove the pizza dough from its package. Slowly stretch the dough on the back of your knuckles, rotating the dough and stretching it into a circular shape. When the dough is stretched to about 1 foot in diameter, place on the work surface and stretch the dough even more using your fingertips.

Place the dough directly onto the middle rack of the oven. Bake until the top of the crust is browned, about 4 minutes. Using tongs, remove from the oven, and place on the work surface with the bottom of the crust facing up. Spread the carrot puree over the flatbread. Scatter the cheese over the puree. Drizzle the reserved cheese marinade over the top. Place the flatbread in the oven, again directly on the wire rack. Bake until the crust is browned and the cheese is melted, 4 to 6 minutes longer. Using tongs, carefully remove the flatbread and transfer to the work surface. Cut into pieces and serve.

Yield: 2 servings | *Prep Time:* 10 minutes | *Cooking Time:* 16 minutes

MUSHROOM AND SPINACH QUESADILLAS

When I'm in a rush and in need of a quick meal, I turn to the mighty quesadilla. While I enjoy the combination of mushrooms and spinach heightened with tomatoes and scallions, you can use any veggies on hand.

2 tablespoons canola oil, divided, plus more as needed

1 (10-ounce) container white mushrooms, sliced

½ teaspoon kosher salt

1 (10-ounce) bag spinach

2 tomatoes, chopped

2 scallions, chopped

2 cups shredded low-fat cheddar cheese (8 ounces)

4 (8-inch) Whole Foods Whole Wheat Tortillas

Preheat the oven to 300°F. Heat 1 tablespoon canola oil in a large sauté pan or skillet over medium-high heat. Add the mushrooms and salt, and sauté, stirring occasionally, until the mushrooms are soft, about 10 minutes. Add the spinach, and cook, stirring constantly, until wilted, 2 to 3 minutes. Add the tomatoes and scallions, and cook 1 to 2 minutes. Transfer the vegetables to a bowl.

Spread ½ cup cheese over each tortilla, covering it entirely. Divide the vegetables evenly, spreading on one-half of each tortilla, and fold the other half of the tortilla over the vegetables. Heat the remaining 1 tablespoon canola oil in a medium nonstick skillet over medium-high heat. Add 1 quesadilla, cooking until each side is golden, about 3 minutes per side. Transfer to a rimmed baking sheet, and place in the oven to keep warm. Repeat with the remaining quesadillas, adding more oil as needed. Cut each quesadilla into four pieces, and serve.

Yield: 4 quesadillas | *Prep Time:* 10 minutes | *Cooking Time:* 35 minutes

BROCCOLI, SUGAR SNAP PEA, AND EDAMAME STIR-FRY

A veggie extravaganza like stir-fry is always a favorite. This one includes edamame for a little boost of protein.

- 1 tablespoon canola oil
- 1 large head broccoli, cut into florets
- 1 (20-ounce) bag frozen 365 Everyday Value Organic Whole Grain Brown Rice
- 1¼ cups frozen 365 Everyday Value Shelled Edamame, thawed
- 1½ cups sugar snap peas
- 2 tablespoons soy sauce
- 1 tablespoon grated fresh ginger
- 2 cloves garlic, minced
- 1 cup cashews, coarsely chopped

Heat the canola oil in a medium sauté pan or skillet over medium-high heat. Add the broccoli, and sauté, stirring occasionally, until slightly soft, 6 to 8 minutes. While the broccoli cooks, follow the package direction to reheat the frozen rice. Add the edamame and sugar snap peas to the broccoli, and sauté just 1 to 2 minutes. Add the soy sauce, ginger, garlic, and cashews, and sauté, stirring constantly, just 1 to 2 minutes longer. Remove from the heat, and serve with the warmed rice.

Yield: 4 servings | *Prep Time:* 5 minutes | *Cooking Time:* 15 minutes

POLENTA BAKE WITH EGGPLANT AND ZUCCHINI

This comforting casserole is a mix of vegetables, cheese, and marinara sauce.

2 teaspoons extra-virgin olive oil

1 medium eggplant, peeled and chopped

2 zucchini, chopped

1 yellow squash, chopped

½ teaspoon kosher salt

¼ teaspoon freshly ground black pepper

1 cup basil leaves

1 tube cooked polenta, sliced

½ pound Whole Foods fresh mozzarella, shredded (about 2 balls)

2 cups 365 Everyday Value Organic Marinara Sauce

Preheat the oven to 400°F. Heat the olive oil in a large sauté pan or skillet over medium-high heat. Sauté the eggplant until soft, 8 to 10 minutes. Add the zucchini and squash, and sauté until soft, 5 to 8 minutes longer. Add the salt, pepper, and basil, and cook until the basil is wilted, 1 minute. Remove from the heat. Line a 9 x 13-inch glass baking dish with the polenta slices (not all may be used). Spread the vegetables over the polenta, sprinkle the cheese over the vegetables, and top with the marinara sauce. Bake until warmed through, about 15 minutes. Serve.

Yield: 4 servings | *Prep Time:* 10 minutes | *Cooking Time:* 35 minutes

DESSERTS

Dessert can be a source of internal conflict—something sweet is called for but brings the associated guilt that comes with the consumption of all that sugar and fat. But, there are ways to enjoy a sweet treat that's not entirely unhealthy. Focusing on fruit is essential because fruit is full of both vitamins and natural sugar. This is why most of the desserts in this cookbook are fruit based, like the shortcake covered with roasted rhubarb and the tropical fruit puree folded into a whipped topping for a semifreddo. If you need a chocolate fix, try the chocolate pudding, where tofu stands in for dairy, making it—dare I say it—almost a good source of protein. These recipes provide ways to satisfy a sweet craving without getting totally unhealthy in the process.

TOFU CHOCOLATE PUDDING PARFAIT

This luscious chocolate pudding is so addictively good that you won't believe that it's—ahem—almost healthy with the substitution of tofu for milk or cream.

1½ cups 365 Everyday Value Semi-Sweet Chocolate Chips

1 (14-ounce) package 365 Everyday Value Silken Tofu, drained

¼ teaspoon salt

2 teaspoons vanilla extract

8 to 10 cookies, 365 Everyday Value All Natural Crème Cookies Chocolate

In a microwave-safe dish, melt the chocolate chips in 45-second increments, stirring at each break, until the chocolate is fully melted, 2 to 3 minutes. Puree the chocolate, tofu, salt, and vanilla in a food processor, until smooth, just 30 seconds to 1 minute. Transfer the pudding to a container, and refrigerate for 2 hours. Meanwhile, seal the cookies in a zippered bag and crush them with a rolling pin to form coarse crumbs. Assemble the parfait in a parfait dish or a glass: Layer chocolate pudding, cookie crumbs, chocolate pudding, and then cookie crumbs again. Serve.

Yield: 4 servings *Prep Time:* 10 minutes

ROASTED RHUBARB SHORTCAKE

Rhubarb takes center stage in place of strawberries for this shortcake. If you have any leftover roasted rhubarb, stir it into Greek yogurt for breakfast.

1½ to 2 pounds rhubarb, cut into 1-inch pieces

grated zest and juice of 1 Ruby Red grapefruit

¾ cup sugar

1 (14-ounce) Whole Foods Angel Food Cake

1 (7-ounce) sweetened light whipped cream

Preheat the oven to 400°F. Place the rhubarb in a shallow glass ovenproof dish. Top with the grapefruit zest, grapefruit juice, and sugar. Bake until the rhubarb is soft, 25 to 30 minutes. Remove from the oven, and stir the rhubarb, grapefruit juice, and sugar until combined. Let cool to room temperature. When ready to serve, slice the angel food cake. Top each slice with the rhubarb, spoon over some of the juice, and top with whipped cream. Serve.

Yield: 4 to 6 servings *Prep Time:* 5 minutes *Cooking Time:* 25 minutes

TROPICAL SEMIFREDDO

Semifreddo translates to "half cold" in Italian, referring to the dessert that is half whipped cream and half fruit or other flavorings. The ultimate summer indulgence, this is one of the easiest desserts you'll ever make, thanks to the fruit purees found at Whole Foods, plus the TruWhip all-natural whipped topping. Use any fruit puree desired; my preference is tropical bars with pineapple, mango, and banana.

1 (10-ounce) package TruWhip, defrosted in the fridge overnight

2 tablespoons orange marmalade

6 (1.75-ounce) Power of Fruit Tropical Bars, defrosted in the fridge overnight

Line an 8 by 4-inch loaf pan with plastic wrap. Put the TruWhip and orange marmalade in a large bowl. Cut off the top of the container for each fruit bar, and squeeze the fruit puree into the bowl. Gently stir the mixture together, and transfer to the prepared loaf pan. Freeze for 4 to 6 hours, or overnight. Slice and serve.

Yield: 4 servings *Prep Time:* 5 minutes, plus time to freeze

PEACH CRUMBLE

You know all the hard work of pitting and slicing peaches for a dessert? Whole Foods has done most of the work for you, and peaches are just waiting to be nabbed from the frozen section. Plus, buying frozen is cheaper than fresh.

$

For the peaches:

24 ounces frozen 365 Everyday Value Sliced Peaches, thawed, drained, and cut into bite-size pieces

1½ teaspoons ground cinnamon

2 tablespoons granulated sugar

For the crumble:

½ cup flour

½ cup rolled oats

3 tablespoons brown sugar

½ teaspoon ground cinnamon

¼ teaspoon kosher salt

½ cup chopped walnuts (optional)

6 tablespoons unsalted butter, cut into pieces and softened

Preheat the oven to 400°F. In a large bowl, toss the peaches with the cinnamon and granulated sugar. Layer the peaches into 6 ramekins about ¾ of the way full. In a second large bowl, stir together the flour, oats, brown sugar, cinnamon, salt, and walnuts, if using. Add the butter pieces and use a fork to fully incorporate the butter into the oat and flour mixture. Next, evenly divide the crumble mixture on top of the peaches in the ramekins. Place the ramekins on a rimmed baking sheet, and bake until the topping is lightly browned and cooked, about 20 to 25 minutes. Let cool slightly, and serve.

Yield: 6 servings | *Prep Time:* 10 minutes | *Cooking Time:* 20 minutes

TWO-INGREDIENT BANANA-RASPBERRY ICE CREAM

Not possible, you say, to make ice cream without an ice cream maker and with just two ingredients? Welcome to the wonder that is bananas, which can be frozen and whirled in a food processor to create a consistency similar to ice cream. And healthy, to boot. If you prefer, substitute Nutella or peanut butter for the raspberry preserves.

3 to 4 ripe bananas, cut into 1-inch pieces

2 tablespoons raspberry preserves

Put the bananas in a shallow container, and leave in the freezer until frozen, about 2 hours minimum. Transfer to a food processor, and add the preserves. Puree until smooth and the consistency of ice cream, 1 to 2 minutes. Serve at once.

Yield: 2 servings *Prep Time:* 5 minutes, plus time to freeze

BROILED PLUMS WITH VANILLA ICE CREAM

A fruit sorbet can be substituted for the vanilla ice cream, if desired. Scoop little balls of ice cream into the center of each cooled plum.

2½ teaspoons sugar
1½ teaspoons ground cardamom
8 ripe plums, halved and pitted
all-natural vanilla ice cream, as needed

Preheat the broiler and line a rimmed baking sheet with foil. Combine the sugar and the cardamom in a small bowl. Add the plum halves to the prepared baking sheet, cut-side up and sprinkle with the sugar mixture. Broil until the edges are slightly charred, 6 to 8 minutes. Let the plums cool slightly, and serve with ice cream.

Yield: 4 servings *Prep Time:* 5 minutes *Cooking Time:* 8 minutes

PINEAPPLE POPS

Popsicles were always a favorite treat of mine as a child. Making homemade Popsicles is very easy and results in healthier and tastier treats than the manufactured kind. If you don't feel like pineapple, substitute any other fruit of choice.

4 cups chopped fresh pineapple (see page 78)

2 tablespoons sugar, plus more as needed

1 cup water

1½ tablespoons freshly squeezed lime juice, plus more as needed

Pulse the pineapple, sugar, water, and lime juice in a food processor until pureed, about 15 one-second pulses. Adjust the flavor with additional lime juice and sugar as needed. Fill 6 Popsicle molds according to the manufacturer's directions and freeze at least overnight. Run the pops under warm water to remove. Serve immediately.

Yield: 6 pops *Prep Time:* 5 minutes

POACHED PEARS WITH LEMON MASCARPONE

Mascarpone is one of those ingredients that I have trouble hunting down. Whole Foods is one of the few places where I know I can always find it. It adds just a touch of richness to these poached pears.

4 large pears
2 cups water
¾ cup sugar
1½ cups freshly squeezed orange juice
1 tablespoon vanilla extract
2 teaspoons ground ginger
1 teaspoon ground cinnamon
¼ cup mascarpone
grated zest of ½ lemon

Peel and core the pears, then trim the bottoms slightly so they sit flat. Add the water, sugar, orange juice, vanilla, ginger, and cinnamon to a large heavy pot. Bring to a boil, and stir to combine the ingredients. Add the pears to the liquid, cover the pan with a lid, and reduce the heat to low. Simmer the pears until tender, about 30 minutes. Remove from the heat, and let the pears cool in the syrup before removing. In a small bowl, combine the mascarpone and the lemon zest. To serve, cut the pears in half lengthwise and spoon the mascarpone mixture into the center of each one.

Yield: 4 servings *Prep Time:* 10 minutes *Cooking Time:* 30 minutes

BANANA BREAD

The magic of this banana bread is that maple syrup replaces the sugar in the recipe. Try to use bananas that are very ripe. If using extraripe bananas, one trick is to puree them in the food processor to get a banana paste, just perfect for the bread. If you have nuts in the cabinet, add ½ cup of them in the last step.

3 ripe bananas
2 tablespoons unsalted butter, melted
1 egg
½ cup low-fat buttermilk
⅓ cup maple syrup
1 teaspoon vanilla extract
pinch salt
1 teaspoon baking soda
1¼ cups whole wheat flour
½ cup coarsely chopped walnuts (optional)

Preheat the oven to 325°F. Coat an 8 by 4-inch loaf pan with cooking spray. Add the bananas to a large bowl, and use a fork to mash the bananas into a paste-like consistency. Add the butter, egg, buttermilk, maple syrup, and vanilla, and stir to combine. Sprinkle the salt and the baking soda over the mixture, and combine. Add the flour, and use a wooden spoon to combine with the other ingredients. Stir in the walnuts, if using. Pour the batter into the prepared loaf pan. Bake until a toothpick inserted into the center of the bread comes out clean, 50 minutes to 1 hour. Slice and serve.

Yield: 4 servings | *Prep Time:* 15 minutes | *Cooking Time:* 1 hour

FORBIDDEN RICE WITH MANGOES

Black rice, more exotically called "forbidden rice," is one of my favorite purchases at Whole Foods. It's nutty and delicious—and better yet, so nutritious due to its whole-grain status. Stir in coconut milk and serve with mangoes for a dessert.

1 cup forbidden black rice
1 ¾ cups water
2 tablespoons sugar
pinch salt
½ cup full-fat coconut milk
3 mangoes, sliced (see page 26)
¼ cup unsweetened coconut

Add the rice, water, sugar, and salt to a medium heavy pot. Bring to a boil over high heat, cover with a lid, and reduce the heat to low. Simmer until the water is absorbed, 30 to 35 minutes. Add the coconut milk, and let the rice sit for 10 minutes. Stir to combine. To serve, scoop the rice into bowls, and garnish with the mango and the coconut.

Yield: 4 servings *Prep Time:* 4 minutes *Cooking Time:* 30 to 35 minutes

S'MORES WITH SEA SALT

Whole Foods makes their own marshmallows, so why not utilize them for homemade s'mores to satisfy a chocolate craving. These s'mores are given an adult twist with sea salt on the chocolate.

½ (12-ounce) bag 365 Everyday Value Semi-Sweet Chocolate Chips

1 tablespoon heavy cream

8 graham cracker squares

sea salt

8 Whole Foods homemade large marshmallows

Put the chocolate chips in a microwave-safe dish and melt in the microwave in 45-second increments, stirring at each break, until the chocolate is fully melted, 2 to 3 minutes. Add the cream to the chocolate, and stir to combine. Cover a rimmed baking sheet with two layers of waxed or parchment paper. Working quickly, dip one side of a graham cracker square into the melted chocolate, using a small spatula or knife to smooth the chocolate on the cracker, if necessary. Repeat with the remaining graham crackers. (If the chocolate gets cold while doing this, reheat in the microwave for 30 seconds.) Sprinkle sea salt on top of the chocolate-covered graham crackers. Put the baking sheet into the freezer, and let the chocolate harden for 1 hour.

Wrap the crackers individually in waxed or parchment paper and place in a zippered bag. Refrigerate the graham crackers until ready to use. To make the s'mores, preheat the broiler. Line a rimmed baking sheet with foil, and put the marshmallows on the baking sheet. Broil until the marshmallows are toasted, about 1 minute. Top each chocolate-covered graham cracker with a toasted marshmallow, and serve.

Yield: 4 s'mores *Prep Time:* 5 minutes, plus time to freeze *Cooking Time:* 5 minutes

MIXED FRUIT SMOOTHIE

This fruit smoothie can be enjoyed for dessert, or as a snack any time of day.

1¼ cups 2% Fage Greek yogurt

1½ cups frozen 365 Everyday Value Whole Strawberries

¾ cup freshly squeezed orange juice

1 banana, cut into pieces

1 tablespoon agave nectar or honey

In a blender or food processor, add the yogurt, strawberries, orange juice, banana, and agave nectar. Puree until the strawberries are broken up and the smoothie is thoroughly blended, 30 seconds to 1 minute.

Yield: 2 servings *Prep Time:* 5 minutes

CONVERSIONS

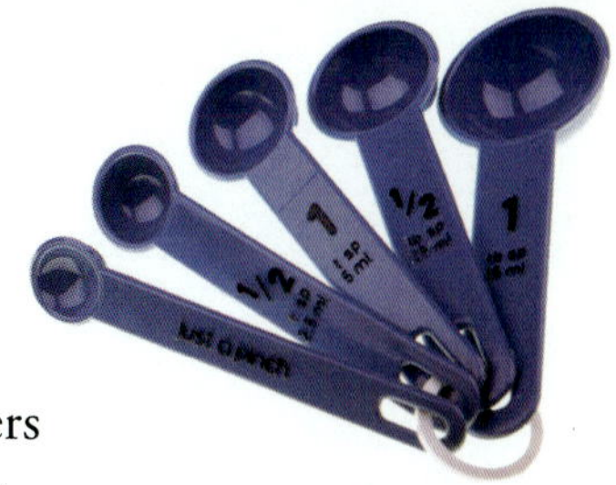

MEASURE	EQUIVALENT	METRIC
1 teaspoon	--	5 milliliters
1 tablespoon	3 teaspoons	14.8 milliliters
1 cup	16 tablespoons	236.8 milliliters
1 pint	2 cups	473.6 milliliters
1 quart	4 cups	947.2 milliliters
1 liter	4 cups + 3½ tablespoons	1000 milliliters
1 ounce (dry)	2 tablespoons	28.35 grams
1 pound	16 ounces	453.49 grams
2.21 pounds	35.3 ounces	1 kilogram
325°F/350°F/375°F	--	165°C/177°C/190°C

PHOTO CREDITS

Page 5: © Eric Gevaert/Fotolia.com
Page 10: © Elena Schweitzer/Fotolia.com
Page 12: © Diana Taliun/Shutterstock.com
Page 17: © tfazevedo/Fotolia.com
Page 20: © mareandmare/Shutterstock.com
Page 24: © Yasonya/Fotolia.com
Page 28: © Edyta Pawlowska/Fotolia.com
Page 35: © jeehyun/Shutterstock.com
Page 39: © Nikola Bilic/Fotolia.com
Page 43: © Viktar Malyshchyts/Shutterstock.com
Page 44: © Alexander Petrov/Fotolia.com
Page 49: © Elenathewise/Fotolia.com
Page 50: © xmasbaby/Fotolia.com
Page 58: © Pakhnyushcha/Shutterstock.com
Page 60: © eyewave/Fotolia.com
Page 64: © volff/Fotolia.com
Page 67 © kayx/Fotolia.com
Page 71: © Imageman/Shutterstock.com
Page 76: © marco mayer/Shutterstock.com
Page 80: © Petr Malyshev/Shutterstock.com
Page 97: © Eldin Muratovic/Fotolia.com
Page 99: © Andreea Szekely/Shutterstock.com
Page 102: © bitt24/Shutterstock.com
Page 104: © kzww/Shutterstock.com
Page 109: © Evgeniy Drogozhilov/Fotolia.com
Page 115: © Zigzag Mountain Art/Shutterstock.com
Page 118: © ivan kmit/Fotolia.com
Page 123: © motorlka/Fotolia.com
Page 128: © matka_Wariatka/Shutterstock.com
Page 133: © Nattika/Shutterstock.com
Page 134: © Valentyn Volkov/Shutterstock.com
Page 138: © marekuliasz/Shutterstock.com
Page 140: © alexmisu/Shutterstock.com
Page 141: © carroteater/Shutterstock.com
Page 143: © Saskia Massink/Fotolia.com
Page 144: © Marco Mayer/Fotolia.com

RECIPE INDEX

A

Angel Hair with Tomatoes and Chickpeas 68
Arugula and Salami–Stuffed Peppadew Peppers 10
Asian-Style Chicken Thighs 82
Asian-Style Fusilli Salad 56

B

Bacon-Wrapped Bananas 16
Banana Bread 137
Bangers and Onion Gravy over Potatoes 92
Beef Fajitas with Red Peppers and Onions 84
Beef Tacos 87
Black Bean Burgers 114
Blackened Catfish Tacos 103
Black-Eyed Pea Dip 17
Braised Beef and Cabbage 90
Braised Chipotle Turkey Drumsticks with Sweet Potatoes 74
Braised Fennel with Oranges and Olives 51
Broccoli, Sugar Snap Pea, and Edamame Stir-Fry 123
Broiled Plums with Vanilla Ice Cream 133
Buttermilk Mashed Potatoes 45

C

Caramelized Onion Dip 21
Celery Root and Apple Puree 42
Cheese Ravioli with Bacon and Peas 67
Chicken and Rice with Ginger Sauce 75
Chicken Cutlets with Fruit Salsa 78
Chicken Marsala 81
Chicken Parmesan 76
Chicken Soup with Crispy Rice 30
Chicken with Jalapeño-Cilantro Sauce 72
Chilaquiles 117
Chinese Chicken Salad 28
Cilantro Brown Rice 54
Cinnamon-Scented Roasted Chicken with Apples 71
Corn Salad 24
Couscous with Dried Cranberries and Pine Nuts 46
Cured Salmon with Horseradish Cream and Crackers 11
Curried Cauliflower with Dried Cherries 50
Cheese Log with Apple Slices 18

F

Fettucine with Lemon Shrimp 58
Flatbread with Carrot Puree and Marinated Goat Cheese 121
Forbidden Rice with Mangoes 138

G

Garam Masala Tomato Soup with Cheesy Flatbread 33
Guacamole with Pomegranate Seeds 20

H

Hummus with Cucumber Slices and Cherry Tomatoes 15

K

Kasha with Spring Vegetables 49
Kimchi Soup with Cellophane Noodles 35

L

Lentil Salad with Mango 26
Linguine with Tomatoes and Eggplant 64
Low Country Boil 104
Low-Fat Creamed Spinach 39

M

Marinated Eggplant with Olives 40
Meatloaf 86
Meyer Lemon Carbonara 65
Mixed Fruit Smoothie 140
Mojo-Marinated Shrimp Kebabs 102
Mushroom and Spinach Quesadillas 122
Mussels with Coconut Milk and Lemongrass 99

O

Orange-Glazed Chicken over Spinach 77
Oven-Baked Hash Browns with Eggs 115

P

Panzanella Salad 23
Peach Crumble 130
Pesto-Stuffed Tomatoes 37
Pineapple Pops 134
Pitas with Baked Falafel and Cucumber-Yogurt Sauce 111
Poached Pears with Lemon Mascarpone 135
Polenta Bake with Eggplant and Zucchini 124

Polenta Casserole with Pork Chops 96
Polenta with Dried Mushrooms..38
Pork Spareribs with Hoisin Sauce 93
Pork Tenderloin with Orange and Fennel Relish.................. 95
Potato Leek Soup 31

Q

Quick-Sautéed Cucumbers with Red Pepper Flakes............ 44

R

Roasted Asparagus with Orange Zest...................................53
Roasted Brussels Sprouts with Mustard Seeds 43
Roasted Rhubarb Shortcake 128
Roasted Tomato Bruschetta 12
Rosemary Focaccia with Roasted Yellow Tomatoes 118

S

Salmon with Honey Glaze... 100
Scallion-Marinated Chicken..80
Scallion Quinoa with Corn and Squash............................ 112
Shepherd's Pie 97
Shrimp with Spicy Cocktail Sauce 13
Smashed "Fried" Potatoes 48
S'mores with Sea Salt...139
Soup with Greens 29
Spaghetti and Meatballs.. 59
Spaghetti with Eggs and Ramps...66
Spinach-Stuffed Shells 61
Spring Greens Salad... 25
Steak in Lettuce Wraps with Pickled Vegetables.................. 88
Spring Rolls...8

T

Tilapia Fish Cakes with Caper Tartar Sauce 108
Tofu Chocolate Pudding Parfait 126
Tropical Semifreddo 129
Tuna-Stuffed Red Bell Peppers 109
Turkey Chili with Beans 34
Turkey Lasagne.. 63
Twice-Baked Sweet Potatoes 119
Two-Ingredient Banana-Raspberry Ice Cream 132

V

Veal Paprikash with Egg Noodles 91

W

White Beans, Pesto, and Shrimp..106
Whole Trout with Roasted Garlic and Preserved Lemon..... 105

Z

Zucchini Pesto Pasta..60

ABOUT THE AUTHOR

ANDREA LYNN, author of *The I Love Trader Joe's College Cookbook*, is a food writer and recipe developer with a culinary arts degree from the Institute of Culinary Education and a creative writing degree from Agnes Scott College. She has worked as a personal chef and as senior editor at *Chile Pepper* magazine. Her articles and recipes have appeared in print and online for numerous publications.